A Villa *on the* Costa Blanca

A Villa *on the* Costa Blanca

ROBERT H V COOKE, FCIS

BT Batsford Ltd London

©Robert Harlan Vivian Cooke 1988
First published 1988

ISBN 0 7134 6034 2

Printed in Great Britain by
Dotesios Printers Ltd, Bradford-on-Avon
for the publishers B.T. Batsford Ltd
4 Fitzhardinge Street, London W1H OAH

Acknowledgements

Many Spanish people have assisted in the compilation of this book in the generous and warmhearted way which typifies their welcome to foreigners, without reservation, as visitors or permanent residents in their country.

In particular, I wish to single out for my special thanks Emilio Salar Gálvez, Gestor Administrativo Colegiado, of Torrevieja, for checking the whole of the manuscript and offering much helpful advice. Thanks also to Emilio Pacheco Gomez, Juan Jose Herandez Pascual and Pilar Trincado Camino, all of the Banco de Madrid, for lucidly explaining the complications of banking and exchange control; to Pedro García Vaillo of Unión Previsora S.A. for information on insurance matters; to Colin Taberner, Secretary of the La Siesta Urbanization Committee, regarding community matters; to John Henry Ricketts for expert horticultural advice, and finally to the *abogados* (lawyers) of the International Law Centre of Torrevieja.

Foreword

This is a most useful and timely book. As the author makes clear, he moved to the Costa Blanca and quickly realised how much he could have known before he arrived.

A Villa on the Costa Blanca is written with a professional eye to the legal and administrative jungle which characterizes Spain today. But it is clear that Spain is changing as she shapes up to her new membership of the EEC and the frontier-free Europe of 1992.

This is good news for *extranjeros*–foreigners–who have moved to Spain or who are thinking of doing so. Already, more than a million foreigners own property there, half of them British.

The problems of buying a property in Spain, or even renting one, are candidly set out in this book. I have been examining this sector for over two years and I have seen much misery among the expatriate community. Almost always, those who encounter problems have been too trusting.

My conclusion is this: before committing any money to property, take professional advice. In the European Parliament we are working hard with the Spanish authorities to squeeze out bad habits, but they die hard.

It is particularly pleasing to see that the author's check-list at the end of the book encourages the potential Costa Blanca dweller to learn Spanish. Do so–it will double the pleasure of living in this lovely country.

Edward McMillan-Scott

Edward McMillan-Scott MEP
(York, Conservative)

European Parliament *rapporteur*
on cross-border property purchases.

Contents

1
Sun, sea and sand

Many British people and other northern Europeans are now seeking the sun on the unpolluted Costa Blanca, whether they rent a property, buy one, or go to live there permanently. The vast majority enjoy themselves immensely. A few encounter personal problems which are so severe that they have to return home, often at a considerable financial loss. Many difficulties arise because people rush to rent or buy without due consideration of all the factors involved. The other major problem for most foreigners is coping with the documentation and bureaucracy, especially if they have little or no command of Spanish. In order to smooth the path as much as possible, this book attempts to show you how to come to terms with the culture shock and to feel at home in Spain.

You do not need to buy or rent a villa to find this book useful; it is similarly applicable to those considering a bungalow or an apartment. The property does not necessarily have to be on the Costa Blanca, as much of the information is relevant to the whole of Spain and its islands; even, in general terms, to many other Mediterranean countries. And finally, you do not have to be British, as most of the laws and regulations apply to all nationalities.

So why the Costa Blanca in particular? It has many advantages and attractions, including some of the best beaches in the whole of Spain, stretching in an almost unbroken succession from end to end, with room to be alone if that is what you want. The Moorish castles are so undiscovered that you are likely to have them to yourself to wander around undisturbed. The climate is as ideal and as healthy as any you are likely to find elsewhere on earth, the summer heat usually tempered by cooling sea breezes. Being on the mainland is another advantage, as it gives you a variety of choices regarding transportation. Originally it was largely undiscovered because communications were only fair, but this is now changing rapidly, with a good airport at Alicante and priority being given to improved roads.

For long the Costa del Sol was the part of Spain which foreigners most favoured for settlement. Here prices of property have escalated so rapidly that even a studio apartment will now probably cost you around £28,000 and you will not have a lot of change out of £200,000 if you buy a custom-built villa. Because the Costa Blanca is only just beginning to be developed, in many areas you can obtain what are undoubtedly real bargains, with a small bungalow available for just under £10,000 and a two-bedroomed detached villa for £17,900. Even so, the amount of available building land on or near the coast is extremely limited in extent and is now rapidly being used up. A similar escalation in prices must soon be anticipated on the Costa Blanca, and those who buy merely as an investment are very unlikely to be disappointed. Early purchasers have already seen a 50 per cent rise in the value of their properties in only two years.

However, those who rush out and buy or rent without giving the matter proper forethought are liable to make expensive mistakes. At very least it could mean a ruined and miserable holiday; at worst it could entail being stuck with a nightmarish property in which you are forced to continue to live because you find it impossible to dispose of it. I have a saying – 'There is one way that is better than learning by experience, and that is learning by other people's experiences – it is less painfull!' - and so my objective is to warn you of the possible pitfalls and try to ensure that your stay in Spain is as enjoyable as possible, however long it may be.

Notwithstanding the above saying, there is really no substitute for first-hand experience, and unless your venture into the Spanish real estate market is exceptionally urgent, my considered advice is:

▶ rent a property for a holiday in the area which interests you;

▶ buy only when you are certain that you are making a good choice,

▶ and make the move to permanent residence only when you are quite sure that you are ready for that considerable change in lifestyle.

This book is arranged in the same sequence as these points, so that the early chapters will be of interest to all groups, the middle ones to all buyers, and the later ones mainly to permanent residents, or those contemplating such a step in the future.

2
The Costa Blanca
- a guided tour

As a brief introduction to what the countryside of the Costa Blanca has to offer, I have devised six routes around the region, which I hope will whet your appetite.

ROUTE A

Alicante - Santa Pola - Torrevieja - La Manga - Cartagena - Mazarrón - Aguilas

Leave *Alicante* by the coastal road to the south, and, just beyond the suburbs, bear left on to the N332 Cartagena road. Pass through *El Altet* village, cross the plain and climb the wooded hill, where you can make a detour to the left to *Santa Pola*. Here at the harbour your can take an interesting boat trip to *Tabarca Island,* which has no proper accommodation for visitors, although there are restaurants, and there is clear water for swimming and diving.

Rejoin the main road under the flyover, then drive through the salt pans (*salinas*) with a wide variety of waterbirds on view, including flamingos at times. (At the top of the rise, the first detour left will take you to *Playa de Pinet.*)

Continuing on the N332, for about 70 km (43 miles) you will run parallel to some of the finest beaches in the whole of Spain, or perhaps anywhere in the Mediterranean area. At *La Marina* the sand dunes are backed by pine woods for shade and a picnic, extending for 16 km (10 miles) to the south. *Guardamar de Segura*, just off the main road, is an attractive town which stages a colourful Moors and Christians festival in July.

Further south you will pass close to extensive expatriate urbanizations before reaching *Torrevieja*, a town with rather undistinguished shops, but an interesting port with salt workings.

Beyond the town there are many more pleasant beaches, often involving a short detour, such as *Dehesa de Campoamor.*

Costa Blanca - South

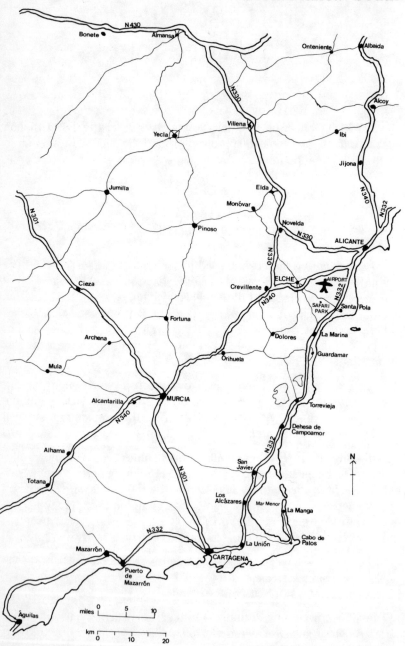

Now cross the border into Murcia province, with flat agricultural plains, and drive through the little towns of *San Pedro del Pinatar, San Javier* and *Los Alcázares.*

Here a rather longer detour is very rewarding around the massive salt-water lagoon of *Mar Menor.* Take the road alongside the southern shore, before forking off right at *Cabo de Palos* to see the tall lighthouse. Continuing north-westwards from *Cabo de Palos,* along the narrow sandspit which separates the lagoon, with its varied watersports, from the beaches on the seaward side, you will come to *La Manga,* a smart modern resort. You can drive a little further, although eventually it is necessary to turn around as the promontory ends in scattered islands. On return you can take an alternative route to either *El Algar* or *La Unión,* before rejoining the N332 to the south.

You will soon reach *Cartagena,* a fair-sized town and an important naval base. It is certainly not short of castles, though the interesting Castillo de la Concepción on the highest point stands out above the others. There are good views from the adjoining attractive Parque de las Torres. Not far below is the Iglesia de Santa Maria Vieja and parts of it are certainly old, including the Roman mosaic floor.

(If you now wish to return to Alicante by a different road, take the N301 to *Murcia,* then the N340 to *Alicante.*)

Route A continues on N332, a sweep inland being necessary as the Sierra de la Muela drops sharply to the sea. After about 30 km (19 miles) you come to the attractive resort of *Puerto de Mazarrón* on the bay of the same name. The town of *Mazarrón,* with its castle and interesting sixteenth-century church, is a short run inland.

Continue through the semi-desert region of the Sierra de la Almenara to the limit of the Costa Blanca at the little town of *Aguilas,* also a resort, which is dominated by its castle.

ROUTE B

Alicante - Elche - Crevillente - Orihuela - Murcia -Cartagena

Route B also begins in *Alicante,* but starts with a short tour of the city first.

Head south towards the harbour and follow the Parque de Canalejas, where drivers will find parking. Continue east under the shade of the palm trees of the Explanada de España until you reach the beach where, on the left, set back from the road, you will see a tunnel which is the

Alicante

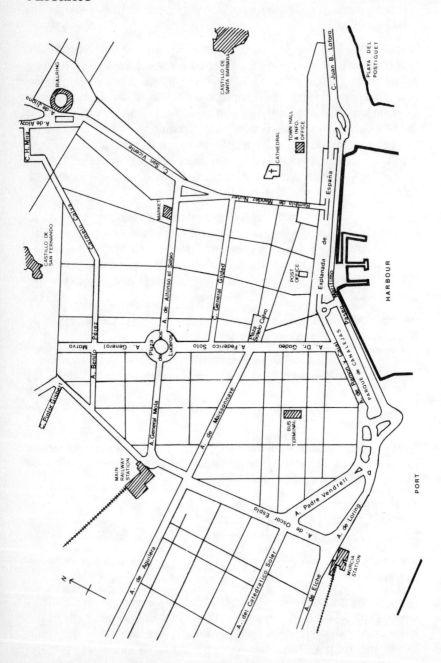

entrance to a lift. Pay the small charge and ascend to the Castillo de Santa Barbara for panoramic views of the city with its harbour and beaches, as well as far beyond. The castle contains a museum.

If you do not mind steps as an alternative return route, leave by the lower gate and take the first turning left off the road down an unsurfaced track where you can descend between the very picturesque old houses, embellished by wrought ironwork and pot plants, of the Barrio de Santa Cruz in the old town. Close by you have the Catedral de San Nicolás de Bari and the *ayuntamiento* (town hall).

Continue west until you reach the wide Rambla de Mendez Nunez, then turn right and go up the rise to the covered market. (Incorrigible view-fanatics can go a little further north to the Castillo de San Fernando, approached by a surfaced road winding around to the back, or by steps from the first track leading off right.)

Make your way up the A. de Alfonso el Sabio back to the Plaza de los Luceros at the intersection of the two main avenues, and you will be convenient to bus, train or car.

Leave Alicante by the same south coastal road as in Route A, but this time fork right on to the N340, and after 23 km (14 miles) you will reach the ancient city of *Elche*.

It has many thousands of palm trees; head for the Huerto del Cura, which is well signposted. Here you will see the palm with seven trunks, as well as a cactus garden along the shady paths.

Now head for the blue dome of the Iglesia de Santa María, where the 'Mystery of Elche', a religious play, is staged in August. Only a short distance beyond is the Alcázar de la Señoría, a Moorish palace with square towers. The Parque Municipal, alongside, is one of the best tended in Spain. A look at the *ayuntamiento* in the city centre nearby can complete the tour.

Leave town on the N340 and head for *Crevillente,* recognizable by its factories which produce nearly three-quarters of all the carpets and rugs woven in Spain. Those interested in sculpture will want to see the Mariano Benlliure Museum in the crypt of the Iglesia de Nuestra Señora de Belén.

A further 22 km (13½ miles) south (and just off the main road) is the small, but historical city of *Orihuela*.

The cathedral of El Salvador is regarded as being one of the best in the region. On the northern outskirts see the old university, which is now the

Elche

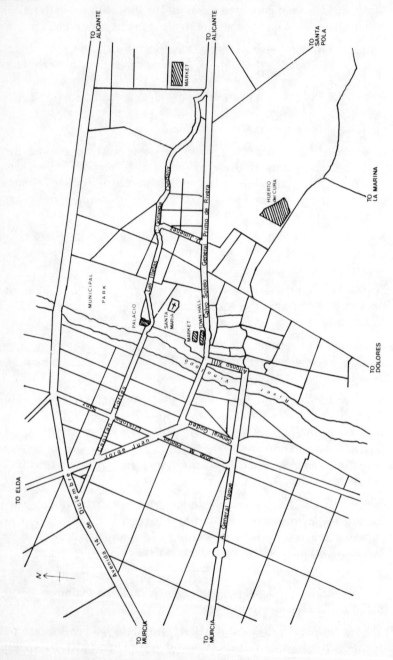

Colegio de Santo Domingo, beside the Puerta de la Olma. Head west to the Calle de Sargent, and from the plaza climb the hill to the Seminario de San Miguel for a panoramic view of the city and its ruined castle.

Murcia, the capital of its province, is a further 22 km (13½ miles) south.

Park close to the Río Segura on the avenues which are a spectacle in spring, with the mauve blooms of the jacaranda trees alternating with orange, laden with ripe fruit.

The Catedral de Santa Maria is the showpiece of the city, with good views obtainable from its north tower. Most of the shops are congregated in the narrow streets around this area (although they are not directed towards the tourist trade) and there are many shady street cafés.

Finally, see the gardens and fountains of the Glorieta de España, close to where the Puente Viejo spans the Segura river.

Take the N301 road, which climbs the Sierra del Puerto before becoming a straight, but interesting, highway across the flat plains to *Cartagena,* (described in Route A - an alternative way back to Alicante).

ROUTE C

Alicante - Novelda - Sax - Villena - Biar - Alcoy - Jijona - Alicante

Route C could well be called the castle circuit. Leave Alicante by the N330 Madrid road, and at 25 km (15½ miles) detour left to *Novelda* to find, alongside the Río Vinalopó, the Castillo de la Mola with a triangular base to its tower. The Sanctuary of La Magdalena is close by.

Back on the main road, the Moorish castle at *Petrel* towers over the old town. A little further along, *Sax* castle can be closely approached by car along a track to the north. This was originally a Roman fortress, built on a knife-edged ridge.

At *Villena* you will see the squat tower of the Castillo de la Atalaya dominating the town, which is a good place for a meal or a snack. The churches of Santiago and Santa Maria are also of interest, as is the Archaeological Museum in the town hall.

Now take a side road 7 km (4 miles) east to *Biar,* where you will find the Moorish round castle. Go through the mountain pass, from where the road is straight to *Ibi;* halfway along, the unfinished castle of Castalla is perched improbably on one side, and that of Onil on the other.

You will soon reach *Alcoy,* which displays a varied skyline of domed churches and derelict factories. You can see the lavish costumes worn during the Moors and Christians *fiesta* on permanent display at the Casal de San Jordi.

Return along the N340, and after 2 km (1¼ miles) a detour right through rugged forests to the *Santuario de la Fuente Roja* is well worthwhile, whether for a picnic, walks, or a spectacular view across the valley to the mountains.

Back on the main road, after 6 km (3¾ miles) a short detour left would take you to the cave paintings at the *Refugio de la Sarga*. The highway twists and turns endlessly to *Jijona*, where you can buy locally-made *turrón* - a sweet of Moorish origin. Soon afterwards the N340 straightens out for the run back to Alicante.

ROUTE D

Alicante - Canalobre - Aitana - Guadalest - Callosa - La Nucia - Benidorm

Route D is along very scenic, but minor roads.

Follow the N340 north through *San Juan de Alicante*, and after another 3 km (2 miles) turn right for *Busot*, where the Cueva de Canalobre is signposted. Besides offering spectacular views from the entrance, this gigantic cave has massive stalagmites and stalactites in floodlit chambers up to 107 m (350 ft) high. The constant temperature of 16°C (61°F) means that a woollen garment can be useful on the hour-long tour.

Return to Busot, and keep bearing left through *Aguas de Busot* and *Relleu* until you reach *Safari Aitana*, one of the largest safari parks in Europe. At *Benasau* turn right for the attractive and unspoiled mountain village of *Confrides*.

Guadalest, a further 10 km (6 miles) on, is certainly well worth a stop. Although far from undiscovered by tourists, the impregnable castle constructed on a rocky outcrop by the Moors is still impressive.

Continue to *Callosa de Ensarriá*, the place to buy honey, there turning right for Polop castle and *La Nucia* to complete the route in *Benidorm*.

ROUTE E

Denia - Pego - Callosa - Benisa - Gata de Gorgos - Jávea

Route E is another mountain tour, although the roads are wider for the second half.

Leave *Denia* by the coastal highway to the west heading for *Pego*, with another safari park about three-quarters of the way along on the right. At *Pego* turn left and follow the very scenic C3318.

On reaching *Orba* you can detour left to *Benidoleig* to see the caves of las Calaveras. Back on the original road, continue between the almond trees through *Tárbena*; 10 km (6 miles) beyond, a narrow track to the left takes you to the Fuentes del Algar, a beauty spot with a 24-m (80-ft) waterfall. You can swim in the pool below, picnic, or use the restaurant.

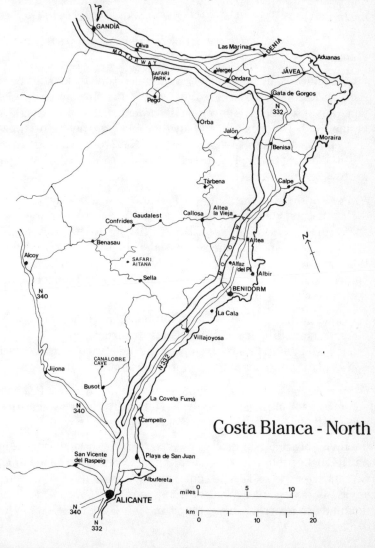

Costa Blanca - North

At *Callosa* turn left for *Altea La Vieja*, and then left twice more to take you to *Benisa*, where there is the Catedral de la Marina. After another 12km (7½ miles) through agricultural land, the twisting road reaches *Gata de Gorgos*, which is noted for its cane and basket-work made from esparto, palmetto, straw and wicker. Here turn right along the short, but interesting, road which takes us to *Jávea.*

ROUTE F

Alicante - Villajoyosa - Benidorm - Altea - Calpe - Moraira - Jávea - Denia

Route F takes you along the coast of the northern part of the Costa Blanca.

Leaving *Alicante* by the road which runs alongside the Castillo de Santa Bárbara, keep bearing right to *Albufereta*. A detour right is necessary if you want to see the little coves of *Cabo Huertas*. Drive past several miles of fine sandy beaches around *Playa de San Juan,* before reaching the rocky promontories of *Campello*. Join the N332 road, which takes you to the little fishing port of *Villajoyosa*, interesting around the lower part of the town.

Benidorm, love it or hate it, now comes into view, with Playa de Poniente to the west and Playa de Levante separated by the promontory on which stands the old part of the town. Besides having two beaches, Benidorm is really two towns with the seasons, the elderly in winter taking over from the young of summer; but whichever season it is, there is sport and entertainment for all. Just off shore is the Isla de Benidorm with its triangular silhouette, reached by boat excursion.

Continue north on the N332 for a further 10km (6 miles) to arrive at *Altea*, its harbour a magnificent sight with a backdrop of stratified and eroded mountains. Climb the steps to the old town and notice the tiled domes of the churches in this picturesque area.

Further up the coast, *Calpe* is unmistakable, the massive headland of Peñón de Ifach jutting out into the sea for you to climb if you are feeling energetic.

Improving beaches and an attractive coastal highway take you to *Moraira* and its rocky promontories. Here it is necessary to turn inland to *Jávea*, with its extensive expatriate community. (Another detour through pine woods is necessary to see the rocky coast at *Cabo de la Nao*, an alternative return route being possible.)

Turn left out of Jávea to continue the scenic route to *Denia*, dominated by the squat bulk of its castle. Beyond, at *Las Marinas*, miles of sandy beaches stretch into the distance.

Benidorm

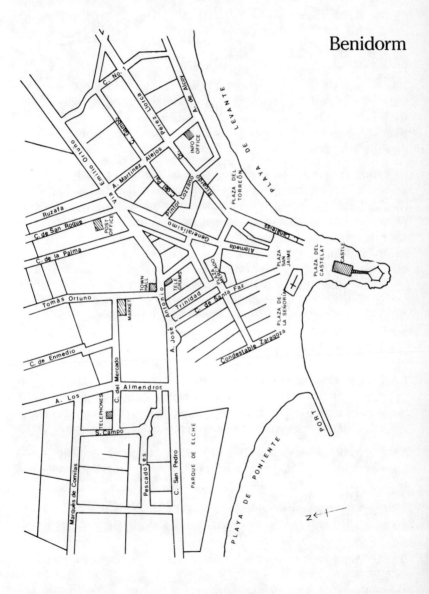

3
Flights and other transport

FLIGHTS

It invariably pays to shop around for flights, because the fares cover a very wide range. For instance, when I was moving to Spain I was quoted from £62 to £135 for a one-way flight. One method is to contact about three different travel agents who advertise low-cost flights in your local newspapers.

Shopping around is now considerably simplified by one call to the Air Travel Advisory Bureau (01-636-5000, or Manchester (061) 832-2000) as they will inform you which of their members are offering the best deals. Be warned, though, that this is not the objective analysis of all tickets on offer that its name implies, but rather an advertising service for paying members, whose fares are not necessarily the cheapest. Their members are mostly discounted ticket offices, or 'bucket shops' as they are called in Britain, which specialize in by-passing the agreed fixed fare structure. You may be offered a scheduled or a charter flight (scheduled means that the plane runs to a fixed timetable throughout the year; chartered means an aircraft which is hired to take a reasonably full load of passengers at busy times). You may be offered a seat on a plane chartered by a tour operator, and these are normally reliable. Be wary, however, of speculative charterers, as these may not be offering you a definite flight, but only the possibility of one if they attract sufficient passengers to make the journey economic. So read the booking conditions with care before you sign the agreement and pay your fare.

If you are able to travel at short notice, the lowest fare is probably a late booking, which is available no longer than three to four days before you travel.

Finally, for persons wishing to have a look at property or a certain area, enquire whether there are any cheap package deals which may suit you.

TRAINS

Trains to and from Spain are normally expensive and I do not recommend this method of travel unless you have special reasons, such as fear of flying, heavy baggage to transport, or the availability of a special low fare.

COACHES

Coaches are probably the cheapest way to travel to Spain if you do not mind this form of transport and have the necessary time available. There is the advantage that you can take rather more baggage than on an aircraft. *Eurolines* coaches are very comfortable and they have links with *National* coaches in Britain from London and Dover. The company also has a comprehensive network through Europe from such points as Paris, Brussels, Amsterdam, Hamburg, Oslo, Stockholm, Helsinki, Berlin, Munich, Venice and Rome. Regular long-distance coach passengers know the value for comfort of an inflatable pillow which fits around the neck. One can probably be found in your local camping shop.

CAR FERRIES AND DRIVING

The only car ferry to be of much interest, apart from cross-Channel routes from Britain, is the Plymouth to Santander route which avoids a tiring crossing of France, although still leaves you with about 800 km (500 miles) to travel across Spain to Alicante. Drivers from Norway have the choice of about five different routes. Most Swedish drivers will select Hälsingborg-Helsingor and Korsor-Nyborg because of the short sea-crossing involved. For the same reason, most Finns will opt for the Turku-Norrtalje or Stockholm routes.

Whether you drive from northern Europe or take an alternative method of travel is dependent on four main factors, some of which you might not have stopped to consider before.

▶ Driving may appear at first glance to be the cheapest method of travel, although when you total all the costs of petrol, ferries, motorway tolls, food and accommodation *en route*, plus the many incidentals, it can be extremely dear.

▶ The number of people travelling in the vehicle is an important factor, and one person is not likely to find it an economic method, unless heavy or bulky luggage is being transported.

▶ If you regard the journey itself as part of your holiday, then you will not mind a slower route; conversely, if you need to arrive in the quickest time possible, then you will almost certainly want to fly.

▶ If you have plenty of time in which to enjoy the trip, then the fact that, once you reach the border of Spain, you still have a fairly lengthy journey to the Costa Blanca (which can be a slow one during July and August) will not be too crucial. Be aware, though, that if one person has to spend many hours at the wheel, this is very exhausting, not to mention dangerous for all the occupants of the vehicle because of fatigue.

4
Renting and letting

Back home you are suffering the usual northern European weather; it is pouring with rain out of grey skies and a chilling wind is blowing. The advertisement for a property to let on the Spanish Costa is so alluring that you conjure up visions of a palatial villa with its own swimming pool, just a short distance away from where the Mediterranean gently laps the private beach. It may well be so, although it will not come cheap.

On the other hand, the advertiser may not tell you that it is a cramped studio apartment on the ninth floor where the lift is often out of order for weeks; the neighbours on one side are noisy all day, and parties got on until after 2 am every night on the other; the flat is hot and uncomfortable; you are a great distance from the sea and the shops, besides which there is no bus service and no telephone to call a taxi...

So, before you rush out and snap up this 'unexpected vacancy', consider the above and other matters relevant to the enjoyment of your stay.

Not for one moment am I suggesting that you forget all about renting a property and go back to that usual package holiday. Many people have become disenchanted with the latter because of bland and unappetizing meals, sleepless nights and lack of freedom.

THE LESSEE

Renting a property gives you a great deal more flexiblity. The basic cost is the rental charge, divided by the number of people using the accommodation, although there are considerable incidental savings on all those meals, snacks and drinks which you prepare yourself at the cost of the ingredients rather than paying restaurant prices.

So, firstly, consider exactly what you expect from your holiday, and it may well be that the disadvantages which I have listed at the start of this chapter may not even trouble you. When you have enumerated your requirements in regard to location, accommodation, facilities, transport, nearby entertainment, beaches, and whatever you feel that you need to make your stay enjoyable, then ask the most searching questions before you rent. Ask for distances to be quoted in miles or kilometres rather than in times, because when the owner says, 'The nearest beach is a quarter of an hour away', he may mean driving his Lancia flat out for the 24 km (15 miles) involved. If interruptions to the water and electricity supplies, together with the noise, dust and sand of construction work in progress, are liable to bother you, then check whether the development has been completed.

THE LESSOR

Not all the problems involved in renting affect the lessee, however; plenty more affect the lessor, whether amateur or professional. Seldom do these owners throw themselves wholeheartedly into letting, because, even if it is only a second residence, they feel it is something personal to them and they are afraid that it will be damaged or destroyed. If they have great difficulty in surmounting this obstacle, it may well be that they will decide to let only to relatives and friends. When the latter are the tenants, it is advisable to take a returnable deposit, as this saves the embarrassment of asking for recompense for breakages and repairs.

AGENTS

Beware of letting agents in Spain, whatever their nationality, as there are many unscrupulous ones about. This particularly applies to agents resident on the urbanizations, as a number of them do not inform the absentee owners about some lettings, and pocket all the rents rather than just the commission. One reliable agency is C & S Management Service, 855 Rosa, Urbanization La Marina (UK telephone 0642-700564). Even agents in your home country may take an uneconomically large proportion of the rental for their varied services. So what alternatives does an owner wishing to let have left?

LETTING YOUR OWN PROPERTY

Back home you may have a large circle of work colleagues or social club acquaintances, and the opportunity to display a card on a notice board. Otherwise, you may need to advertise, and then the prospective tenants are likely to be unknown to you. In that situation, if you fear the problems mentioned above, then you could follow the lead of commercial organizations who wish to target their advertising to a particular socio-economic group, and select the publication accordingly.

With this method of letting you may need local support, which is simplified if you have friends living nearby in Spain who are prepared to hold the key, wash the sheets and do whatever else is necessary. The alternative is to let on the basis of 'no linen supplied'. This may be preferable to leaving the key with casual acquaintances, resulting in unauthorized use or even permanent squatters. Value added tax (I.V.A.) of 12 per cent of the value of services (such as the provision of linen or cleaning) should be charged to tenants, because failure to collect this tax may result in the liability passing to you. The *delegación de hacienda* will give you information on how to account for this tax.

LEGAL PROTECTION

This brings me to the question of what protection Spanish law affords to owners and tenants. The first point is that the protection applies only to contracts made before June 1985, and also to tenancies when the term is unspecified, such as from month to month without a termination date. The provisions of the old law extend not only to Spaniards, but also to all residents in Spain irrespective of their nationality. Such tenants can be removed by court order only if they have committed one of nine offences listed in the Ley de Arrendamientos Urbanos.

Tenants protected by the law applying to contracts made before June 1985 have the option of an extension if the agreement is for a fixed period of over one year, even if the agreement states otherwise, except in some listed circumstances where the landlord's need for the property is greater than the tenant's.

Finally, the owner can only increase the rent if the fixed term agreement permits this, and then only by a percentage officially authorized, based upon changes in the cost of living index.

Giving notice to the tenant may involve a delay of at least sixteen months before the owner can regain possession, or it may involve paying compensation to the tenant of one year's rent.

An agreement

Consequently, to avoid all these legal pitfalls, it is preferable to let only to non-residents for a short period and with a written agreement. To be absolutely certain, you could have a Spanish lawyer prepare the latter, although if you draw up a document yourself headed 'Temporary Letting for a Fixed Period' (*Arrendamiento de Temperada*), this should be perfectly adequate, providing that you include all the relevant details:

▶ the names and addresses of the owner and the tenant (each so described)

▶ a statement that it is an agreement to let a property (specify precisely) and contents for a stated period (quote dates) at a rent of £- per week, which includes the cost of gas and/or electricity

▶ an agreement by the tenant to pay a deposit of £-, and an undertaking by the owner to refund this sum on the conclusion of the tenancy, less the cost of any repairs or replacements occasioned by the tenancy

▶ an undertaking by the tenant not to assign or sublet, to keep the property and its contents in good order and to leave everything neat and clean

▶ an inventory

▶ signatures of both owner and tenant, with a date to the agreement

Since June 1985 fixed term tenancies have definitely ended on the stated expiry date.

On agreements made after June 1985 the law gives more protection to the landlord. The previous tight control on rent increases is relaxed, and landlords now find it easier to obtain a court order for the eviction of sitting tenants when the agreement has expired.

5
Local transportation and communications

BUSES

Obviously in a book of this length it is not practicable to list all the timetables of the public transport services in the Costa Blanca region. However, all the major bus routes for longer distances radiate from the main bus terminal in Alicante. - north along the coast as far as Denia, inland to Alcoy, Elche and Murcia, as well as south through Torrevieja to Cartagena. To give you an idea of frequency, here are the number of services operated each working day in both directions from Alicante.

Alicante airport	14	(from 7 am to 10 pm)
Denia and Jávea	4	
Benisa	11	
Altea and Calpe	12	
Benidorm	14	
Alcoy	5	
Santa Pola	23	
Elche and Crevillente	15	
Orihuela	2	
Murcia	16	
Torrevieja and Cartagena	8	

These are summer schedules, so services may be less frequent to some resorts out of the peak season. The above is not an exhaustive list, as there are some connecting links such as Elche to Torrevieja and Guardamar, although buses are not frequent. Fares are very reasonable, averaging around 5 pesetas to the kilometre. Again, it is impossible for me to list services from individual urbanizations to the nearest town, not only because there are so many of them, but also because they are developing and changing rapidly where new construction is taking place. There may be no buses, or possibly a service only during July and August, so you will need to make local enquiries.

TRAINS

Railway lines are quite limited in extent. There is a narrow-guage line from Alicante north through Benidorm and Altea to Denia. The main line runs inland for Madrid and Barcelona, and there is a separate line to Murcia. Consequently, Alicante has three railway stations. On the standard-guage lines services are fairly infrequent, except to Murcia.

On the longer distance routes it is usually necessary to reserve a seat in addition to buying a ticket. Arrangements can be made through travel agencies.

CAR HIRE

If you hire a car locally, expect to pay from £55 to £90 per week according to season for a small Panda or Fiesta. There may be special promotions at quiet times. A larger car will be about £5 to £8 more.

The cheapest I have found for a Panda in summer is £52 per week (plus 12 per cent tax) from Ancla International, Diego Ramirez 152, Torrevieja, telephone 571-6416. They deliver and collect from Alicante airport.

Generally there are few problems and most difficulties arise when hirings are arranged in your home country. So when you pay your hire charge in advance, check that there are no additional costs in Spain. One new resident paid around £80 for one week's hire to a well-known travel agency in England, only to be asked for another £80 by one of the two internationally-recognized hire companies for various 'charges'.

I was not surprised to find a local charge for a tank full of petrol, although I did object to being asked for 50 per cent more than the cost of the maximum amount of petrol that the tank was capable of holding.

More detailed information on buying and driving a car in Spain will be found in Chapter 13.

COMMUNICATIONS

To be perfectly frank, telephone and postal services are not good on the Costa Blanca. Spain will have to make a concerted effort to improve these facilities now that the country has joined the Common Market if it is to be regarded as an industrialized state in the forefront of economic activity.

It is easy to be critical, coming from countries which have had a good infrastructure of such services for a long period, so that small additions are easily installed.

The big problem for the Costa Blanca has been the rapidity of the development, with towns like Torrevieja growing to four or five times their original size in just a few years. As a result, owners on some of the newer urbanizations are having to wait a year or more before they can obtain a telephone. This is a worry for elderly people subject to heart attacks and other illnesses requiring urgent medical treatment, not to mention being a problem for those engaged in business.

Legitimate excuses have been made for the telephone difficulties: the postal delays are, however, quite indefensible. A typical transit time of three weeks to and from the Costa del Sol is ridiculous. A recent build up of 200,000 letters in the Alicante sorting office was due solely to poor planning and organization.

One day my post did not arrive and I did the postman the injustice of thinking that it was because it was raining and he did not want to get wet on his motorcycle. His excuse was that he was new and he could not find the urbanization, although it is the largest in the area and covers several square miles!

When the Spanish postal authorities accept the postage for transit of an item then it seems reasonable that they should deliver it, and not expect you to collect from a central point, or go to the Post Office for large items.

Many foreigners have difficulty in operating the telephones in call boxes, so here are a few hints. The machines take 5, 25 and 100 peseta coins, which you do not press in but merely leave on a slide to drop in on connection and during a call.

The minimum charge for a local call is 10 pesetas, so you can have two 5 peseta pieces first on the slide for such a call. For all other calls within Spain it is best to commence with two 25 peseta coins, and for international calls two 100 peseta coins.

Numbers within Alicante province originally had six figures; early in 1987 the digit 5 was added to the front of all numbers.

To make a call to another province you need to commence your dialling with the provincial code. These are usually listed in the instructions. Here are the most popular ones.

Barcelona	93
Granada	958
Madrid	91
Málaga	952

Murcia	968
Seville	954
Valencia	96

British numbers can be obtained by direct dialling. The procedure is as follows. Dial 07, wait for the tone, then dial 44, followed by the complete British number (omitting any commencing zero on the area code). Therefore, for a London number use 1 and not 01.

Calling Spain from Britain you dial 01034, followed by the area code (excluding the initial 9) and the number. The full area code for Alicante province within Spain is 965, so from Britain you just use 65.

For people living on urbanizations where there will be a delay of years in installing telephones, there is a quick solution available which very few realize. This is by the use of Citizens' Band radio utilizing AM equipment, which is perfectly legal in Spain and of low cost if purchased locally. However, it does need safeguards to prevent the wavebands becoming overcrowded, and untrained operators ruining the vast possibilities.

I hope that bodies such as urbanization committees and community aid organizations will set up study groups to allocate wavelengths and establish priorities for the training of residents who could benefit enormously from the use of their own CB equipment. They would need to be instructed not only in the technicalities of the equipment, but also in the jargon, the ethics and the etiquette of operating CB radio. Given this knowledge, you can well imagine the enormous benefits available to business people, the bedridden, those requiring emergency call facilities, and the depressively lonely, to name but a few, not necessarily in order of priority.

6
Food and drink

RESTAURANTS

The Costa Blanca restaurants span the whole range, from the family kitchen type to the most luxurious. The classification system uses a sign with a number of forks, from one upwards. This designates the quality of the facilities and shows the approximate price level. It is not necessarily any indication of the excellence of the cooking.

Spaniards eat a hearty, not to mention leisurely, lunch, which new arrivals often find too substantial in the heat and following a cooked breakfast. The set lunch, *menú del día*, is often very good value at around 500 pesetas for three courses, plus bread and a passable wine. Alternatively, you can pick at varied *tapas*, as the tasty morsels in bars are called.

The set meal is seldom available in the evening, when you are likely to have to pay around 700 to 1000 pesetas for the main course in a moderate establishment.

MENUS

Local dishes to note begin with *gazpacho*, a chilled and piquant vegetable soup which is ideal to start with on a hot day. A thick soup is *michirones*, made from sausage, ham, peppers, paprika, beans and other ingredients. Many stews are available, such as *pebereta talladeta*, for which tunny steaks are used. *Paellas* abound everywhere; the local speciality, *paella alicantina*, contains crab, octopus, prawns and mussels.

Seafood is the paramount cuisine of the region, with an amazing variety to offer. Particularly well known are *calamares* (squid), sole, red mullet, spiny lobster, and prawns of various sizes, not to mention the humble sardines for a budget snack. The local people eat far less meat than fish, although all the popular meat dishes are available on most menus. Young animals are the basis for *cochinillo* and *cabrito asado*.

Desserts are often a little unimaginative, although this is well compensated for by the sheer range of fruit available and the excellence of the ice-creams.

FOOD PRICES

Which foods are expensive and which are cheap to buy in the shops? Certainly all tinned foods are dear, as well as imported packaged items, instant coffee and some cuts of meat. Green vegetables, with the exception of stringless beans, are expensive during the hot weather. Local tea is of extremely poor quality. Chicken and fish are good value, although the latter should not be kept out of refrigeration for long in summer. Other good buys are all kinds of fruits and vegetables grown locally, particularly if purchased at weekly open air markets.

Here are some current typical prices in summer 1987 per kilo (2.2 lb).

Grilling steak	950 ptas
Pork chops	505 ptas
Leg of lamb	910 ptas
Chicken	234 ptas
Potatoes	30 ptas
Tomatoes	84 ptas
Onions	60 ptas
Frozen hake	680 ptas
Margarine	364 ptas
Butter	889 ptas
Sugar	120 ptas
Plums	80 ptas
Melon	110 ptas
Grapes	100 ptas

Knowing the exchange rate is about 200 pesetas to the pound sterling, you can convert to a British equivalent per lb by dividing the above figures by 440.

ALCOHOL

Alcoholic drinks are very cheap in Spain, including spirits and most liqueurs. The beer is of quite good quality, a popular brand being San Miguel. Some of the local spirits and liqueurs, such as Spanish brandy, are not quite up to the standard to be found in France and elsewhere.

This is not true of the best wine, which comes from the Rioja region and carries a small stamp on the bottle, as this will compare favourably with the very best of other countries. 200 pesetas can buy you a bottle of very drinkable wine from this region.

The Costa Blanca has its own wines, the best begin Monóvar, Pinoso, Villena and Benejama. Red Jumilla is 18 per cent proof. The local Moscatel is a good dessert wine.

Naturally the sherries come from the Jerez region to the south. The domestic champagne is not legally entitled to carry this name and a lot is produced of rather low quality. For the best ask for *cava*.

You can make your own chilled *sangría* by mixing red wine, brandy, mineral water, fruit juice, sugar and sliced oranges with apple, peach or other fruits.

SOFT DRINKS

Many of the well-known brands of non-alcoholic drinks are made under licence. Also widely available is *granizado*, in which natural fruit juices are mixed with crushed ice. Personally I make my own lemonade at home, as lemons are exceptionally cheap.

A local drink to try is *horchata*, a chilled mixture of almonds, cinnamon, lemon peel, sugar and water.

7
Entertainment

Organized entertainment on the Costa Blanca is not really well developed at this stage, except around tourist centres such as Benidorm. Of course, there are discotheques everywhere in places of any size, though opportunities for other types of dancing are fairly limited. Sports are quite well catered for, and these are detailed in Chapter 25 for the benefit of both residents and visitors.

So what entertainment is there?

CASINOS

You can dress smartly and go to a gambling casino. The Casino Costa Blanca at Villajoyosa is rated No. 3 in the whole of Spain. You will need your passport, and the entrance fee is 600 pesetas for the night. Roulette, blackjack and *punto y banco* are available, besides the usual slot machines. The Azar Menor is another casino at La Manga.

NIGHTCLUBS

Nightclubs tend to be congregated mostly around the Benidorm area and you can often see a good flamenco floorshow.

PARKS

Benidorm also has amusement parks, such as Europa Park on the Avenida de Europa.

Acquaparks are becoming very popular (particularly for families with children) and one of the best is to be found on the outskirts of Torrevieja. The cost of 1200 pesetas for adults and 800 pesetas for children aged 3 to 11 may seem quite a high sum, although it does provide a full day's entertainment for the kids, with its water shute, swimming pool with waves, toboggans and waterfalls.

Safari parks

Any of the three safari parks in the region are well worth a visit. These are at Vergel (near Denia), Aitana (in the mountain range inland of Benidorm) and Rio Safari (on the Elche to Santa Pola road).

FIESTAS

These festivals are a Spanish way of life, so you have quite a good chance of encountering one, even on a short visit. If you see flags and decorations in the streets, then make local enquiries.

The most colourful are the *Moros y Cristianos fiestas*, which are impossible to list here as they take place in 46 different towns, and often the dates are movable, so check with your tourist office. The outstanding one is at Alcoy around April. At Denia and Jávea the historical reconstruction takes the form of an attack which takes place from the sea.

Rather different is the *Hogueras de San Juan* in Alicante around the 24th June, which includes the burning of giant effigies. The *habaneras* musical festival is held at Torrevieja in August.

BULLFIGHTS

You may dislike bullfights as much as I do, but perhaps it is desirable to see just one to gain an undertanding of the Spanish way of life. The Spaniards themselves are far from unanimous in supporting bullfighting. Because of the high cost of staging bullfights, they are held on a regular basis in the Costa Blanca area at only Alicante and Benidorm.

AT HOME

For indoor entertainment it is necessary to rely on radio and television, unless you have a video. More details of these are given in Chapter 25, as likely to be of much more interest to residents than to visitors.

8
Selecting a property

SMALL, MEDIUM OR LARGE?

Probably the most important factor in deciding where to buy is the price, because your geographical preference may well be out of your budget range, and you will have to adjust your expectations accordingly.

Most people with a property to sell in Britain will find an equivalent one on the Costa Blanca at lower cost, and they will have a balance left over to invest, subject to settlement of any outstanding mortgage. Those selling in the London area and the south-east will have considerably more left than northerners.

So with all this money to spend, should you choose the most expensive villa that you can afford, one in the middle price range, or the smallest property suitable for your use?

There is no one simple answer, as various factors have to be taken into consideration, such as whether you are buying for capital appreciation, the maximum rental income, for your own occasional use or permanent residence, and whether you expect to have relations and friends to stay on a frequent basis.

If you are buying as an investment, you should be aware that the resale property market in Spain is exceedingly slow, because with so many new houses being built most buyers prefer one which has not been lived in by someone else. Of course, you can turn this situation to your advantage by buying a resale cheaply.

For the greatest capital appreciation, my advice is to buy close to a pleasant beach where new construction or redevelopment is unlikely to obstruct the sea view. There is now a ban on building higher than six floors in Alicante province.

If you want to maximize your rental income, then look at properties from the view of prospective tenants, who will consider the accommodation charge per person, that is the rental divided by the number of people that it will sleep.

If it is just going to be a holiday home for your occasional occupation, then it will not matter if it is small, as you are likely to spend most of your time out of doors.

For permanent residents, however, the claustrophobic feeling of cramped accommodation could prove intolerable. Occasional visitors can be accommodated in the living room on a bed-settee, although this is far from ideal on a regular basis, and a property with a second bedroom is probably better value if you can afford it.

So, in general, what would be the best choice after allowing for the above considerations? At the risk of seeming conservative, I personally would choose the middle price range. The problem which you may face if you decide to sink all your available funds into one expensive property is that, should living costs rise sharply, then you could hardly dispose of part of it to finance an increased level of spending, as you could do with more liquid investments.

In addition, there are few buyers at the top end of the market, whilst the demand is considerable for lower-priced accommodation, consequently forcing up the cost at frequent intervals. However, these properties are mostly apartments and terraced bungalows which have many disadvantages from the point of view of permanent residence. When this factor becomes more generally known, I think that prices will stabilize to some extent.

And so we are left with the middle range, perhaps typically the detached two-bedroomed property which many developers rather grandly call a villa, but which is probably more accurately termed a chalet. Naturally, as the cost of smaller properties rises, this, in turn, forces up the price of the middle range to preserve the differential. Apart from this factor, I believe that in the medium term the main demand will be for such properties in the middle range.

THE COST

To add some flesh to the bones of these arguments, let us look at the typical prices we should expect to pay on the Costa Blanca in 1987, depending upon whether the property is close to the sea or a few miles inland.

	Beachside	Village
Apartment, studio	£9,500	-
Apartment, 1 bedroom	£15,500 to £30,000	-
Apartment, 2 bedrooms	£22,000 to £37,000	-

Bungalow, 1 bedroom	-	£9,500 to £14,000
Bungalow, 2 bedrooms	£38,000	£13,500 to £17,500
Chalet, 2 bedrooms	-	£18,000 to £23,000
Villa, 2 bedrooms	£46,500	£32,000
Villa, 3 bedrooms	£86,500	£24,000 to £38,000

Beachside apartments will vary considerably in cost, depending not only on size but also on exact location and view. In the above prices bungalows are terraced, chalets and villas are detached.

LOCATION

There figures will show you just how much prices are affected by location. Your desire to be close to the sea may be a wish that you find affordable or not.

The most important factor which you need to take into account in connection with location is whether you intend to have your own **transport,** because with it you are likely to have few problems except the cost of running a car. Without it, consider your typical week and the journeys you are probably going to need or wish to make, and to what extent these are likely to be possible and convenient by the available public transport. Even walking a mile to the nearest bus stop can be extremely tiring in the heat of summer.

Aspect is important for a number of reasons. Obviously you will want to look out on to a pleasant scene rather than a brick wall, although you should consider what could possibly intervene in the future as a result of further construction.

Sunlight/shade is certainly a vital factor, and different people will have contrasting opinions on this matter, besides which you will have to balance the requirements of summer and winter. A west-facing well-shaded property will barely receive any direct sunlight in winter. My own preference is for a south-easterly aspect, which provides morning sunlight in winter, which is the time when you need it most.

You are likely to spend a lot of time on your **terrace,** so consider whether you will be looking at about five other families doing likewise, whilst they look back at you, able to hear and observe your every word and action. This is more likely to happen in terraced bungalows built in straight lines, front facing front. Alternate properties facing in opposite directions are much better from this point of view, as are staggered rows.

NEIGHBOURS

Spanish people are very friendly and hospitable, although it can be an acquired art living next door to them in connecting properties on a permanent basis. One family often seems to make more noise than a whole street of other nationalities, with their loud radios and television, shouting rather than talking, and dogs which bark incessantly at every passer-by, whether day or night.

Permanent residents and holidaymakers seldom mix well as neighbours, because the former look for a quiet night and the latter do much of their sleeping on the beach by day, and so are very active until around 2 am. There is no reason why you should not enquire about your prospective neighbours, if they are known, before you purchase.

FACILITIES

Next consider what facilities you require on a regular basis. Obviously this will be a much more important factor if you are going to be a permanent resident, as you are likely to have a great deal of spare time on your hands if you are not working. You may be very active and need the availability of tennis, golf, or walking near at hand. Find out what bars, restaurants, shops for your daily and occasional use are conveniently situated nearby.

A swimming pool, whether shared or private, may or may not be important to you. My own observations indicate that few people with private pools make very much use of them, and I doubt whether most owners obtain economic value from them. They do not come cheap, even small ones with barely room to turn. A shared pool encircled by a limited number of properties is often available reasonably cheaply.

Water seems to attract screaming children, however, so elderly residents should bear this in mind if they are likely to find it wearing on their nerves.

Apart from sports clubs on urbanizations having pools on a subscription or daily charge basis, there is now great pressure upon developers to provide such recreational facilities free to all residents.

AGE OF PROPERTY

Should you purchase a new or a resale property? A large proportion of prospective buyers would not even consider the latter. However, resales have some advantages and they should not be completely ignored.

Resales

Bear in mind that the foundations have had time to settle (earth tremors are far from unknown in Spain) and any faulty construction work should be beginning to show. Modern Spanish properties are not subject to very much wear and tear internally, consequently showing little sign of previous occupation. The frequent annoyances of development work in progress are a thing of the past, and your neighbours are established and known. Last, but not least, you are very likely to buy at a bargain price, though you must make certain that the deeds are in order.

New developments

If construction work is in its early stages on the urbanization (or one of its phases), be aware that you are likely to suffer many annoyances. These will almost certainly include water and electricity being cut off (possibly both at the same time) for periods of up to two days in duration. Sand and dust will blow everywhere throughout the house. Piledrivers, ditch diggers, cement mixers and construction vehicles will assail your ears with their various noises. This work tends to be extended over a considerably longer period when prospective buyers select a particular plot before any building takes place, resulting in piecemeal development.

If you are present in the area during construction, refuse to allow broken air bricks to be used, as these have an adverse effect upon insulation.

INSPECTION FLIGHTS

These low-cost trips are a fine idea if you are fairly certain that you want to purchase from one particular developer. If you wish to shop around, then forget them, as the organizers have a vested interest in ensuring that you have no opportunity to do so.

In the former case they are good value, as the trip is subsidized, all transport is provided (which could be costly if you had to hire taxis) and the schedule makes the best possible use of your limited time for the three or four days involved. Generally no pressure is exerted to buy.

EXHIBITIONS

Exhibitions in your home country are often of fairly limited value, although they do give you the opportunity to obtain much more information than is generally available from a brochure, typically including videos, large-scale maps, a^e `al photographs, site plans and, of course, the valuable facility of bein le to ask questions of knowledge-able staff.

ESTATE AGENTS

There are some estate agents in Britain and other northern European countries which handle or specialize in Spanish property, although they mostly concentrate on the more expensive end of the market.

In Spain you will find them by the sign marked *Inmoblaria,* and most offer the complete range. Do not necessarily rely on them to keep you informed of properties coming on to the market after you have returned to your own country.

It is unusual for estate agents handling a sale to fix their sign. The Spaniards' way of selling is generally not to employ agents, but to paint the words *Se Vende* with a telephone number for contact. So if you are touring around an area which interests you, then it is quite likely that you will see this marked somewhere on properties. Occasionally you may see a For Sale sign in English.

ADVERTISING

Newspapers in Spain carry advertisements for a wide selection of properties for sale. If you are unable to arrange for a friend living locally to send you copies or cuttings, then they are available on subscription. The *Costa Blanca News* (Apartado 95, Benidorm [Alicante]), will be posted to European addresses for six months at a cost of 5855 pesetas ordinary mail, or 6455 pesetas air mail. The *Entertainer,* which has separate Costa Blanca, Almeria and Costa del Sol editions, can be obtained for a similar period for 2000 pesetas by sending your cheque (payable to Paperweight S.A.) to Apartado 414, Garrucha, Almeria. The cost is the same for the *Costa Blanca Post;* make your cheque out to Pisapapeles S.A., and send it to Apartado 2071, Benidorm.

TIME SHARE

Time sharing has acquired a bad reputation recently in Spain, due to aggressive American marketing techniques in which husband and wife (the most common purchasers) are separated and virtually locked in until they sign an agreement. This apart, there is no reason why you should not buy a time share if you like to go to the same place at the same time each year. Companies offering exchange facilities with other time shares throughout the world offer greater flexibility.

There are two main points that you should bear in mind. Firstly, you need to consider whether you are really buying your share at an economic rate, particularly as service charges tend to be extremely high. Secondly, you should take just as much care in obtaining legal advice as if you were buying a property outright, as you could lose your money if the time share company has a defective title, or outstanding mortgages which it is unable to meet.

Time share properties are not particularly widespread in the Costa Blanca at present, except in attractive areas where land is extremely limited, such as on the narrow sandspit separating the massive Mar Menor lagoon from the sea. If you can find about twelve other interested buyers, there is no reason why you should not form your own timeshare group.

9

Purchasing a property

Having considered the factors mentioned so far, and any others that are relevant to your particular circumstances, you have now definitely decided to buy your dream house in the sun.

THE AGREEMENT

The developer or seller will now ask you to sign a contract, which is an agreement for sale, and to pay a deposit, which is non-returnable if the buyer declines to proceed. There is no reason why you should not ask for the *contrato* to include a clause to the effect that the deposit will be returned if the seller has a defective title, or is responsible for non-completion.

Do note that this agreement is binding and unlike the procedure in Britain where the parties agree 'subject to contract'. So if the sale of your property back home falls through, and you do not have the necessary finance available at the appropriate time, then you could lose your deposit as well as stage payments.

Where a property is being built in Spain, it is usual for the agreement to provide for payment by stages, typically: 10 per cent deposit; 40 per cent within one month of contract; 25 per cent three months before completion, and the remaining 25 per cent on completion. The Spanish equivalent of VAT (called IVA), currently set at 6 per cent on property, is generally required with stage payments.

It is highly desirable for the contract to include a penalty clause for late completion, as most Spaniards have no conception of the importance of time. If the contract states that the penalty clause is invalid if the buyer is late in making any payment, take the greatest care to be on time and have proof of the date on which you make payment. Some developers deliberately date receipts up to a month late and then contend that your payment was not on time.

THE SOLICITOR

Before you sign any agreement or pay any money you should insist on consulting a Spanish solicitor *(abogado)*, first ensuring that he is not also acting for the seller. Sales staff may put difficulties in your way, but if they see that you are quite determined about this (and you should be) then they will afford facilities.

Your solicitor will generally know what is required to protect your interest. However, you should specifically ask him to ensure that the agreement is fair to you, that the seller has a good title to the property, and that a 'foreign money contribution' will be officially recorded in connection with your payments. The necessity for the latter is because Spain has exchange control regulations, and if you later decide to sell for pesetas, a document will be required to enable you to transfer these funds out of the country.

When the solicitor has satisfied you that everything is in order you can proceed, making payments as necessary until completion.

FURTHER COSTS

When selecting a property which you can afford, it should be borne in mind that various taxes and charges are involved. It is prudent to allow about 12 per cent of the purchase price if you are expected to meet all of them.

The largest single item is likely to be IVA, assessed at 6 per cent on the purchase price, and often collected by instalments with stage payments as mentioned above.

Connection charges for water and electricity are likely to amount to around £270, plus a further £37 if you have a gas contract.

There is a fee for registering the property in your name, and this is based on its official value, which is generally much less than the purchase price.

The purchaser is liable for *impuesto transmisiones* (transfer tax), also based on the official value and currently levied at 0.5 per cent on new properties and 6 per cent on resales. This registration is carried out by a *notario*, who prepares the title deeds *(escritura)*. Spanish law states that his fee, again based on the official value, is payable by the seller. If the latter does not pay (and it is usually passed on) then the purchaser is liable. Allow about £600 for notarial legal fees, preparation of the deeds and property registration.

Finally there is the urbanization charge to the Community of Owners, which will probably be around £60 per year, unless it is a small community with lavish facilities. If you are on a tight budget, there is no need to obtain your *escritura* and register the transfer into your name immediately, although it is not advisable to delay these matters for long. Absentee owners can arrange for a Spanish resident of any nationality to complete these formalities with the *notario,* as long as this person is appointed by a deed called an *escritura de poder de compraventa.*

Some months after the *escritura,* a tax on the increase in land value (commonly called *plus valía*) is collected by the municipal authorities. Again it is a legal liability of the seller which is usually passed on to the buyer. It is assessed on the official land value (excluding buildings) on a sliding scale from 0.5 to 2 per cent, depending upon how many years have elapsed since the land last changed hands, between up to 5 and 50 years. This will probably amount to around £150 on the popular properties.

Depending upon the terms of your contract, at completion you should arrange insurance of your property and its contents.

You will require sufficient funds in your Spanish bank account at completion to meet all these charges and taxes. Bear in mind that foreign cheques take approximately one month to clear.

INHERITANCE TAX

Before you rush off to the *notario* to register the property, consider whether it would be preferable to put the ownership in the names of your children, and obtain from them an agreement allowing you to occupy it rent free for life. The reason for this is that the rates of Inheritance Tax are quite high in Spain and they commence at a much lower level than in Britain. The necessity for the agreement, however much you trust your children, is that you will have to produce proof to the authorities that you have a permanent place to live when you apply for periodical residence permits. Spanish law does not recognize nominee owners, and whoever is registered is regarded as the true owner. Consequently, it is not advisable for non-relatives to be registered as the owners of your property.

FINANCE

Mortgages and loans to purchase property in Spain are possible both from British financial institutions and from Spanish banks. In the former case, British investments or property will be required as security for the loan. Spanish banks can make the loan, with official permission, to enable you to purchase from a resident Spaniard a new property on which a mortgage secures the loan. Foreign currency must be the source of the funds used for repayments.

10
Furnishings

THE COMPLETE PACKAGE

If you are purchasing a new property from a developer, it is quite likely that he will offer a complete furniture package. There are various pros and cons regarding acceptance.

The **advantages** include the convenience of a single purchase for new owners who have very limited time available before they need to occupy their property. Generally, workers drill holes for wall furniture, fix light fittings and hang curtains - all jobs which can be time-consuming and expensive if you have to search for assistance. The developer knows from experience the exact requirements of each type of property.

The package tends to be good value for money, as the developer is making a large single sale and buying at wholesale prices. In addition, he usually offers various free items which could cost quite a substantial amount in total.

The main **disadvantage** is that the packages lack individuality and per-sonality, so that many people may feel that living in nearly identical houses, all furnished in exactly the same way, may seem like too regimented a form of living. Developers are usually flexible regarding some alterations to the standard package, and you may like to consider my compromise idea of buying an alternative three-piece suite, as this can completely transform the 'package look'.

THE COST

Furniture is certainly not expensive in Spain and you are sure to find it cheaper than in your home country. It should be possible to furnish any property adequately for about 10-12 per cent of the purchase price. Even so, you should not lose the opportunity of negotiating discounts with furniture showrooms when you are spending substantial sums or buying large items. A 10 per cent deduction should be obtainable, but check the normal price in advance of negotiation to ensure that you are really receiving a deduction.

INDOOR FURNITURE

A few comments about Spanish furniture may help you to avoid expensive mistakes.

Many beds are made with wooden slats, so specify springs if you prefer them. Test mattresses for comfort before you buy, as many are very solid. There is not much difference in price between an ordinary sofa and a sofabed, which can be very useful for unexpected guests.

Spanish dining chairs are often extremely uncomfortable when made of wood or metal.

Many refrigerators do not have a drip tray, so check to avoid pools of water on the floor. Because of this problem, and storm water coming in under the back door, it is advisable to have plastic legs for standing kitchen fittings.

If you use olive oil for cooking, it tends to spit a lot, consequently covered frying pans and cooking pots avoid a lot of greasy cleaning.

Bear in mind the possibility of perspiration stains on chairs, choosing your patterns accordingly and considering the options for cleaning and washing.

Finally, remember that there is usually a lot of dust and sand in the air and dark woodwork tends to show up every speck.

The Spanish climate will almost certainly affect your furnishing plans. Obviously you will require far less bedding than in colder climates - duvets being preferable to blankets and heavy bedcovers. The other main difference which you will notice is that you will require far fewer carpets and rugs than back home. It is a good idea to take these up in summer, as they are subject to heavy wear upon tiled floors. When storms threaten leaks under doors, this is another time to take them up.

TERRACE FURNITURE

If you are coming from northern Europe you may not appreciate just how important your terrace will be as the living room where you will spend most of your day and evenings as well. The comfort of your terrace furniture should therefore be one of your primary considerations. This can be the case in winter as well as in summer if you fit sliding or folding glass panels to use the sunshine instead of incurring heating costs.

The final point to make about furnishings is that strong and simple furniture is very desirable if you intend to let your property, particularly if strangers are to be the tenants. When equipment is provided for their use, it is advisable to leave clear operating instructions in English or their native language.

IMPORTING FURNITURE

The cost of transporting furniture from your home country to Spain tends to be excessive in relation to its value. Generally speaking, it is better to sell your furniture before leaving and to buy new in Spain. Even so, there are likely to be smaller items and personal effects which you will want shipping out.

The necessary documentation for importing to Spain is simplified considerably if you are able to wait until you receive your *residencia* (residence permit). Then you are permitted to import small items free of duty, as well as furniture, decorations, clothes, bicycles, very small motorcycles, musical instruments, and books, providing that all these items are for your own use. Duty is levied on new electrical items, so if you have purchased them recently, take them out of their boxes and fit plugs, even though you will probably have to change the latter in Spain.

If you import before obtaining a *residencia,* then a bond will almost certainly be required. No doubt you will want the latter returned to you at the earliest opportunity, and (as the requirement is to show the intention of becoming a permanent resident) the Customs Authorities will probably be satisfied with the official acknowledgement that you have made application for a *residencia,* plus your *escritura* or house contract.

In all cases, obtain a number of quotations from removal firms, as charges vary enormously, and check with friends which companies are familiar with the documentation required. This involves detailed lists in duplicate (plus a Spanish translation) signed by the owner. The lists have to be stamped by the Spanish Embassy in London or in your home country. A declaration will be required from you that you have not resided in Spain previously and that during your first two years in Spain you will advise the local Customs Office of any change of address, and will not sell the goods.

For those with a holiday home retained solely for the owner and his family, the position is slightly different. Used furniture and equipment can be imported without taxes or duties being levied. In this case, the undertaking is that the items will be used only by the owner and his family, they will be kept in the same property for two years and they will not be sold. This document requires the stamp of a Spanish Embassy or Consulate General, and it is likely that a bank guarantee will be demanded. Obviously this exception does not apply to properties which are rented out.

In either case, ensure that the carrier knows when the items are required in Spain, as part loads can take a long time before they fill a vehicle.

11
Ongoing costs

Apart from the cost of living of food and drink, which will vary enormously depending upon your lifestyle, it may be wise to budget for annual costs such as urbanization charges, rates, water, electricity and gas. Absentee owners can probably arrange for their bank, *gestor* (legal executive; see Chapter 19) or solicitor to pay most or all of these charges. In fact, there is a legal requirement for a non-resident property owner to appoint a resident of any nationality as his tax representative to deal with fiscal matters. Taxes vary according to personal circumstances, and these are covered in Chapter 15.

URBANIZATION CHARGES

These are payable to your local Community of Owners to finance the facilities which they provide to residents on the development. An annual levy is usually collected by the Treasurer, and it will probably amount to around £60 per year.

RATES

Rates payable to the municipal authority are considerably lower than in Britain. It is not possible to give a precise figure, as it will vary not only with the value of the property, but also with the area in which it is situated, but a sum of about £40 per year would be reasonable in a village development. Recent rises have been most pronounced in large municipalities which provide public transport (such as the urban area of Alicante), and least in country villages with few facilities.

The initial notice will be sent to you, and it is necessary to pay this in person at your local town hall *(ayuntamiento)*. Subsequently, a standing order can be made for settlement by your bank. Late payment involves a 20 per cent surcharge, and the date on which it is due varies from September to November according to locality.

WATER

Water charges are metered, so they will vary according to usage. It is not suggested that you give up washing, but economies can be made: vegetable water can be used for the garden, if this consists of only a small border, whilst a brick in the toilet cistern can reduce the volume of water used, without affecting the flushing effectiveness.

Certainly you would find a lawn expensive to maintain in this hot, dry climate with a very porous soil. Water costs around £1.60 per cubic metre, so allow £55 per year, including the standing charge.

ELECTRICITY

Electricity at 50 pence per kilowatt hour costs about the same as in Britain per unit, so this should not be an expensive item, providing that you do not use it a great deal for heating in winter. £85 per year should suffice. The main saving which you can make is by switching off your water heater at night and when you are out for long periods and not using it. Standard demand is only 3 kilowatts, and you have to pay an extra £75 and a higher two-monthly charge if you require more power.

The one major disadvantage to electricity is power cuts. Far too often in rented accommodation, power cuts have meant that I have had to make do with a cold salad in the evenings when I was hungry for a cooked meal, or (which is far worse) suffered loss of power when the meal was half cooked. Also, the switches have a habit of tripping themselves if you use the oven and rings for cooking at the same time. When you lose power, it is not even possible to make a hot drink. Keep a torch plus candles and matches handy, as cuts tend to last for many hours.

Also note that a minimum charge is levied for electricity every two months, even if none is used. Consequently, owners making frequent short visits may decide to rely on electricity, and residents may consider purchasing a cooker on which the rings are half electric and half gas.

GAS

Gas is available in cylinders and has two main advantages over electricity: it costs only about one-third of the price in Britain, and it is not affected by power cuts.

A spare cylinder is supplied as part of a gas contract, so you are never without means of cooking and heating. A gas cylinder costing around £3.60 should last about 3 months with average usage.

SWIMMING POOL MAINTENANCE

Annual running and maintenance costs for swimming pools shared with a number of other properties are generally fairly low. For private swimming pools the ongoing costs are normally in proportion to the size of the pool. Obviously you can make savings by discontinuing use of the pool during those months when the weather is seldom suitable for its use.

INSURANCE

Finally there is your house and contents insurance, with premiums about £1.75 per £1000 on the former, and £6.25 per £1000 on the latter. If you are not a pensioner, health insurance is obligatory in order to obtain your *residencia*. Costs are given in Chapter 17.

12

Permanent residence

OBTAINING A *RESIDENCIA*

If you intend to become a permanent resident in Spain, the first step you should take is to obtain a special visa from a Spanish Embassy or consulate in your home country before leaving. Your letter asking for an application form to be sent by post is liable to be ignored unless you enclose a stamped addressed envelope. It is obligatory to deliver your application in person, although the visa can be posted on the following day if you prefer not to collect it.

In London the Spanish Consulate General is at 20 Draycott Place, London SW3 2SB, which is quite near to Sloane Square underground station. My advice is to arrive very late in the morning, unless you want to wait for three or four hours to hand in the application, which is merely accepted and stamped. Perhaps this is a deliberate test to see whether you are likely to withstand the bureaucracy which lies ahead! In England there is also a Spanish consulate at 1A, Brooks House, 70 Spring Gardens, Manchester 2.

A passport valid for 5 or 10 years is essential. When you arrive in Spain, ask for your passport to be stamped with an *entrada* date stamp, as the immigration authorities often do not bother to do this during the busy tourist season. Shortly after arrival you should register with and obtain a certificate of good conduct from the consul of your country. On the Costa Blanca they are at present located at the following addresses:

Belgium	Avenida del Catedrático Soler 8, Alicante
Denmark	Plaza Calvo Sotelo 3-7C, Alicante
Finland	Calle Gambó 3, Benidorm
France	Virgen del Socorro 39, Alicante
Netherlands	Rambla Méndez Núñez 58, Atico, puerto B, Alicante
	Ed. Cervantes, Avenida de Europa, Benidorm
Norway	Avenida Ramón y Cajal 3, Alicante
	Ed. Aurea 6° A & B, Calle Pal No. 1, Benidorm
	Calle Diana 27, Denia
Sweden	Avenida Ramón y Cajal 3, Alicante

UK	Plaza Calvo Sotelo 1, Alicante
USA	Rivera 3, Valencia
W. Germany	San Francisco 63-4, Alicante

The special visa allows you to stay in Spain for 90 days, and if you intend to become a permanent resident it is advisable to start collecting the various documents for a *residencia.*
You will need:

▶ your passport with a special visa, together with a photocopy of each page up to and including the special visa

▶ certificate of registration with your consulate

▶ certificate of good conduct from your consulate

▶ five passport-type photographs

▶ a photocopy of your house contract or *escritura;* if you are not buying a property, then a long-term tenancy agreement will be required

▶ evidence of means to support yourself

▶ a photocopy of a health insurance policy with a Spanish company, if you are below pensionable age, or a certificate in Spanish that your foreign health policy gives cover in Spain; pensioners need a form of confirmation from a health authority in their country of origin, plus registration with the Spanish Health Service at Calle Churruca 26, Alicante (which is near to the main bus station)

▶ tax stamps of c.500 pesetas per person, which are obtainable from your *estanco* (state tobacconist); the exact amount of the *papel del estado* required depends upon nationality

All the above have to be taken in person to the appropriate Policia Nacional office, which for the Costa Blanca area is located in one of five different towns, according to area of residence: Denia, Benidorm, Alicante, Elche, and Orihuela. You can arrange for a *gestor* to deal with these matters if you feel that your knowledge of Spanish is too limited.

The document which causes the most problems is the evidence of means. The police are not concerned with your funds in other countries, and are only interested in the amount which is being transferred to Spain. Consequently the evidence will normally consist of a letter from your Spanish bank confirming that a sum is transferred to your account each month (at present a minimum of £250 for a single person, or £360 for a couple) and that you keep a 'reasonable' balance. No figure is specified for the latter, and it does not have to be high.

If your pension is transferred to Spain at regular intervals then you will have few problems. Others are recommended to make a banker's order on their home bank and obtain from them written confirmation that the sum specified will be transferred each month to their Spanish bank for the credit of their account.

Spanish banks normally insist on receiving the first payment before giving the required document, and this may take up to one month. It may take up to a further two months before the *residencia* is ready for collection, possibly from the police office in a town close to where you live. You will be given written confirmation of your application, and this can be produced to the police if necessary, should your visa expire before your *residencia* is prepared.

The first residence permit lasts for two years, or a shorter term. Later you can apply for a second *residencia,* which is normally granted for an extended period. Similar documents are required, except for a visa and the certificates from your consulate. Naturally you can cease to be a resident at any stage on returning your *residencia* to the police. Watch your tax position and try to time the change to your best advantage (see Chapter 15).

OBTAINING A *PERMANENCIA*

If you wish to stay in Spain for more than 90 days, and you are unable or unwilling to become a resident, then you will need to make similar quarterly applications for a *permanencia.* The documents required are as for a *residencia,* with the exception of the certificate of good conduct and the health insurance policy. A bank balance of at least 210,000 pesetas is required for one person, or 230,000 for a couple. In some provinces (not in Alicante) one or more *permanencias* are required before you are permitted to apply for a *residencia.*

ADAPTING TO SPANISH LIFE

Now if you want to make a success of your new life in Spain, more is required from you than merely obtaining a residence permit. You have to come to terms with a different culture and adapt to a different lifestyle. Try to prevent yourself from making comparisons, and from thinking that your way of doing things is 'right', and the Spanish way 'wrong', because Spain is not going to change; you are the one who is going to have to make adjustments. This 'culture shock' can affect you dramatically, or hardly at all, depending on how open-minded you are; but until you accept things as they are, you will never feel 'at home'.

Try not to continue reading only newspapers containing domestic news of your country of origin. Attempt to learn Spanish and something about your new country of residence, because local people will be appreciative of any effort you make. And try not to confine your social life to groups of your own nationality who spend all their time making unfavourable comparisons, because you will just make yourself unhappy as a result. In short - think positive, not negative!

YOUR RIGHTS

Although you have now obtained a *residencia,* this does not mean that you have changed your nationality. However, you have acquired all the rights of Spaniards in their own country, with the exception of being able to vote, and there is even a move afoot to change this last impediment. Of course, any foreigners can apply for Spanish nationality, but only after they have lived in Spain for ten years.

PENSIONS

If you have already qualified for a British retirement pension, you have the option of having it paid to you in Spain every 4 weeks, or quarterly, or to your UK bank, savings account or agent. Unless you need the whole of this pension in Spain for living expenses, or to prove evidence of means for a *residencia,* it is useful to have funds abroad, as Spain has exchange control restrictions and there are limits on how much you can take out of the country for holidays. Similarly, those in receipt of an occupational or government pension should consider payment within the British Isles. There is no legal requirement as a resident for all of your income to be remitted to Spain.

If you have not yet reached retirement age and you are not working in Spain, you will need to decide whether you should pay voluntary contributions to qualify for a full pension. You need full contributions in only 90 per cent of the tax years of your working life. Your local DHSS office will tell you the percentage of the full pension for which you presently qualify and how many more full year contributions are needed to secure full benefit. It is really an actuarial computation, but by taking an average age to which you hope to live, you can then come to a decision. Of course, you will bear in mind your respective incomes before and after retirement age. Remember that if you are not working you need not pay contributions between the ages of 60 and 65, as you will receive credit for these years.

Once abroad you should correspond with the DHSS Overseas Branch, Newcastle upon Tyne, NE98 1YX.

PETS AS RESIDENTS

It is a comparatively simple matter to bring domestic pets from Britain into Spain without quarantine, and any veterinary surgeon authorized by the Ministry of Agriculture can make the arrangements. The certificates need to be legalized by the Spanish Consulate General in London.

If you do bring pets into Spain, be certain that you intend to stay, as there is a long quarantine period for re-entry into Britain and heavy penalties for attempting to smuggle them through. Many pets have to be destroyed, as their owners have left them in Spain.

13
Buying and driving a car

SPANISH-REGISTERED CARS

As a resident, this is the type of car you will have to drive. The relative costs of an identical new model in Britain and Spain will depend upon the exchange rate between sterling and the peseta at any one time. However, due to various taxes you will probably pay at least a few hundred pounds more at present by buying in Spain.

Secondhand cars

Secondhand cars are more expensive in Spain than in Britain, mainly because they have a longer life expectancy. The roads are not salted, as there is no ice on them in winter, and consequently there is little rusting of chassis and bodywork. Although few cars are garaged, there is rarely any rain for much of the year.

How much will you have to pay? Small cars are much in demand because of their ease of parking on the street in towns, and also because most people cover quite short mileages, so that comfort is not a problem. A locally-built car with a good reputation is the Ford Fiesta, and a four-year old model would probably cost you about £2400 at the present time. A similar one about eight years old would fetch around £1400. Most dealers give a three or six months guarantee on engine and gearbox.

The price can vary a fair amount, depending upon where you buy. For instance, you will buy more cheaply in Alicante, where the main demand is for new cars, than in Torrevieja, where most people want used ones.

Vehicle testing has been introduced for cars over 12 years old, and the test certificate is displayed on the windscreen. It is not quite so easy as in Britain to tell the age of a vehicle from its registration, as each province allocates the latter on an independent basis. The prefix indicates the province, as A for Alicante. The suffix gives a guide to the year, because in Alicante the letters T and U were used for 1979, and in later years the sequence continues with AB, AC and so on, more than one group being used in a year.

BUYING A CAR

When you buy a car, whether new or secondhand, your ownership has to be registered at the regional office of the Jefatura Provincial de Trafico. In Alicante the office is situated on the Avenida Federico Soto, one block up the rise from the large department store Galerias Preciados. You can return after one hour to collect the documents, when the details have been processed through the computer.

Before registering the car, you must pay the tax at the office of the Hacienda in Calle Pintor Lorenzo Casanova. Quite likely you can persuade the seller to accompany you to solve any language problems. The transfer will cost you about the equivalent of £75 on a small car.

DRIVING A HIRED CAR

If you are driving a hired car and you have not been resident in Spain for more than one year, in addition to the documents supplied by the hire company, you will need only a current international driving permit, or your home licence with an official translation into Spanish, obtainable only from your consulate in Spain, a Spanish consulate in your home country, or the Real Automóvil Club de España. Similarly, a permit or licence with translation will be required by a tourist driving a car registered outside of Spain, plus passport, registration book for the vehicle, and confirmation that your insurance has been extended to cover driving in Spain. The latter may not be necessary if you are coming from a Common Market country, but check with your motoring organization or insurance company.

DOCUMENTATION

For a resident driving a Spanish-registered car the following are needed:

▶ *tarjeta de inspección tecnica de vehiculos* (the car's identity document)
▶ *permiso de circulación* (road licence)
▶ receipt for the payment of the current year's tax
▶ driving licence (see below)
▶ certificate of insurance for third-party cover from a Spanish company, with a receipt for the current year's premium
▶ spare wheel and tyre, together with the equipment to effect a change
▶ spare lamps and necessary tools

The documents must be carried at all times and these need to be originals, not photocopies. It is advisable to keep the latter at home in case the originals are lost.

SPANISH DRIVING LICENCE

Residents must obtain a Spanish driving licence if they habitually live in Spain and before they continuously do so for a year. Unless you are fairly fluent in Spanish, it is probably advisable to contact a *gestor* to deal with the formalities. You will require for your first application:

▶ four passport-size photographs (only two required for EEC nationals) each endorsed on the back with your full names and the number of your residence permit, or passport if you have no *residencia*

▶ your *residencia*

▶ a current driving licence issued in your home country, plus an official translation (for non-EEC nationals only)

▶ for non-EEC nationals only, a medical certificate obtained from one of the various centres which have been set up for drivers

INSURANCE

It is obligatory to obtain insurance cover for third-party risks. Annual premiums are presently around £75 for a small car and £100 for a medium-sized one from companies such as Apolo of Alfonso X el Sabio 34, Alicante. Very few people seem to take out more extensive or comprehensive cover. The main reasons seem to be the very high cost and the difficulty of obtaining settlement of claims from many insurance companies.

Apart from insurance, repairs and maintenance, annual costs are likely to be very low, as taxes are only about £20. Petrol at 78 pesetas a litre is roughly the same price as in the UK.

IMPORTED CARS

Imported vehicles can be used by tourists in Spain for a total of up to six months in any calendar year; there are heavy fines for overstaying this period. Drivers should ensure that their passports are stamped on every entrance and exit.

Foreign-registered vehicles can now be imported by future residents free of customs duty and changed to a Spanish registration, providing that the correct procedure is followed. The application must be made when you become a resident, so tell your *gestor* that you wish to do this not later than when the *residencia* application is submitted. You will require a letter from an official body in your home country, such as your town hall or local police force, stating how long you have lived at your last address (which must be a minimum of one year) and the date on which you left to emigrate to Spain. This free importation is called a *franquicia aduanera.*

DRIVING IN SPAIN

Traffic rules and signs are generally very similar to those in your own country and they are largely based upon common sense and safety. Where a lower limit is not indicated, the maximum speed outside built up areas is 90 kph, unless there are hard shoulders or two lanes, when it is 100 kph. A margin of 20 kph is allowed for overtaking slow-moving vehicles. Of course, traffic drives on the right.

Seat belts must be used in the front of a vehicle on the open road, although they are not mandatory in towns and villages. My recommended road map for the area is the Firestone T.28.

14
Local employment

First let me offer a word of warning: if you intend to go to Spain with insufficient income on which to live, depending upon local employment to balance your budget, then research the position *most carefully* before committing yourself to irrevocable steps such as purchasing a property. Spain has massive unemployment and consequently does everything possible to protect the interests of its own nationals. The situation varies from province to province, and with it varies interpretation of the regulations.

WORK PERMITS

On the Costa Blanca the authorities are extremely strict in administering the rules, and work permits are very difficult for foreigners to obtain if they wish to work for someone else. Do not assume that because you intend to be self-employed then you will not need a work permit, because this is often not the case. Those who think that work permits will no longer be necessary now that Spain has joined the Common Market have a long wait ahead of them. As a condition of entry, Spain negotiated that it would retain the requirement for work permits until 1992! However, the regulations will probably be relaxed over a period on a gradual basis.

The professions almost always require a work permit. In some instances, particularly in connection with financial services such as insurance, there is a legal requirement to register. Check the regulations with a lawyer, as an agent needs to register, although a sub-agent does not.

If you are going to be employed in Spain, then normally your employer will obtain a work permit for you. Others really need the assistance of a *gestor,* unless their command of Spanish is very good, as the difficulties are quite formidable. The following documents will be required:

▶ a valid passport

▶ an entry visa if you intend staying over 90 days

▶ five coloured passport-type photographs

- ▶ a certificate of registration with your consulate
- ▶ details of your qualifications for self-employed work
- ▶ a medical certificate from the Spanish Health Authorities
- ▶ a certificate from the Ministerio de Trabajo in appropriate cases that no Spaniard is able to do the work, plus the contract of employment and two further photographs

An application for a work permit is invariably combined with a request for a residence permit.

WORKING ILLEGALLY

Many foreigners work illegally in Spain without work permits, particularly in the seasonal businesses connected with tourism. There is always a demand for people who speak foreign languages as receptionists and agents to deal with the expatriate community and possibly introduce business on commission. These are risky undertakings because you can be imprisoned, fined and deported. Previously the police could force you to leave the country within 72 hours without any right of appeal. The law has just been changed and now the police cannot expel you without first bringing you before the court.

If you are considering working without a permit then you should know about *denuncia*. If a Spanish person reports you to the police for acting illegally, such as working without a permit, then the officials will almost certainly take action against you. In Spain it is almost impossible to keep your employment secret.

EXCEPTIONS TO THE RULE

There are some instances where you can work on a self-employed basis and not require a work permit. These are mostly connected with the arts in the widest sense of the word: writing, music, painting pictures, small-scale handicrafts at home. Remember, however, that your urbanization may have rules preventing you from using your property for business purposes.

STARTING YOUR OWN BUSINESS

Should you plan to set up a business, then remember that you will require a licence from the municipal authorities, and they often ask for very large sums. The licence fee may seem reasonable in relation to the expected profits of the business, but do your cash flow calculations carefully, as this is an outlay which has to be met *before* you make any sales.

The municipal authorities may expect the employment of a certain number of Spaniards in the business as a condition of granting the licence. Spanish wages are generally low, although you should remember that there is a legal requirement to pay an extra month's wages in July and December.

There is an obvious advantage in owning the business premises in which you are going to operate, if you have the necessary capital, although persons starting new businesses in rented premises are quite well protected by the *Ley de Arrendamientos Urbanos:*

▶ rent rises cannot be more than the amount officially permitted in line with cost of living increases

▶ the tenant has an automatic right to renewal of the lease if the conditions have been observed and the rent has been paid

▶ the tenant may assign the lease to a purchaser of the business, providing that the landlord is given a prior option to buy back the lease on the same terms.

Purchasers of existing businesses in rented premises should, however, take the greatest care and seek detailed legal advice. In the latter case the *Ley de Arrendamientos de Industria* contains the relevant law. Briefly, the main problem can be that there is no legal right for the tenant to a renewal of the lease on similar terms, or at all. The latter may therefore be faced with a choice of being held to ransom by a landlord demanding an excessive rent, or surrendering the valuable goodwill of a business without recompense.

TYPES OF BUSINESS

The smallest form of business organization is an *Empresa Individual,* or sole trader, with unlimited liability for debts extending to their private property.

One or more partners in a *Sociedad Comanditaria* may have limited liability, providing that they are 'sleeping' partners.

A *Sociedad Colectiva* is a normal partnership in which the partners have unlimited liability.

A private limited company (or *Sociedad de Responsabilidad Limitada*)

may not have a capital in excess of 50 million pesetas, which may seem a lot, but is less than £250,000.

There is then a very considerable step upwards to the public limited company called a *Sociedad Anonima*.

— 15 —
Taxation

Many people have the reduction of the high levels of taxation existing in their own country as one of their main reasons for moving to Spain. Whether or not this is so in your case, there is no reason why you should not use your position as a Spanish resident to the best advantage in reducing your tax deductions. The improvement does not necessarily come automatically, and it may require careful financial planning on your part.

There is space in a book such as this for me to give only the general principles of British and Spanish taxation. Remember that every individual's tax position is different and it is often advisable to take professional advice, particularly if large sums are involved. A tax consultant will charge a fee, although some financial advisers will give free advice as part of their service.

BEFORE LEAVING THE UK

There are two things which you should remember before you leave home. One is to write to your local Inspector of Taxes telling him the date on which you intend leaving. The other is to delay taking any capital gains (such as selling profitable shares) if at all possible until after you become resident abroad.

There are more details about this later, but first it is necessary to explain *domicile, residence* and *ordinary residence,* as they are defined for British taxation purposes, which is not necessarily the same as understood in ordinary speech. It has been said that a far greater sin than over-simplification is over-elaboration. So, rather than lose you in the complications of the British tax system, I intend to risk the former sin.

DOMICILE

Put very simply, wherever you may be living domicile for this purpose is generally the State which you regard as your 'own' country, although the tax inspector may have different ideas about this. It may change throughout your life from a domicile of origin to one of dependence or one of choice.

Of origin

At birth you normally acquire the same domicile as your father, which is not necessarily the same as either his or your residence, nationality or passport at that time.

Of dependence

A domicile of dependence may be acquired by a child or a woman on marriage. If a woman married before 1st January 1974, she acquired the domicile of her husband, but if the ceremony was on or after that date, she does not change her domicile solely as a result of marriage.

Of choice

A child under sixteen takes any new domicile of the parents on a provisional basis. When the child reaches 16 this becomes a domicile of choice, unless steps are taken to re-establish the domicile of origin or a different domicile of choice.

A domicile of choice is by far the most difficult to attain, because you need to produce irrefutable evidence to the Inland Revenue that you have severed all your ties with your country of origin. This does not necessarily preclude an occasional short visit, although the retention of even one club membership would be enough to deny a change of domicile.

Inheritance tax

The reason why domicile is important is because it normally decides in which country your worldly possessions, wherever situated, are subject to inheritance taxes. If the value of your estate is not likely to exceed £90,000 then there is little point in attempting to change your domicile, as it would be exempt from British inheritance tax. However, note the provisions of Spanish inheritance tax, which is payable on all property in Spain at the death of the owner, irrespective of domicile or residence at that time.

RESIDENCE

Residence is basically defined as where you live for more than six months in a tax year. As you know, the British fiscal year runs from 6th

April to 5th April, although in Spain it is the same as the calendar year. Legally, if you spend 183 days or more in Britain in a fiscal year, then you are regarded as being resident for the whole year. However, by concession, the British Inland Revenue normally divides the tax year into periods of residence and non-residence.

Even if you spend less than 183 days in the UK in a fiscal year, you may still be liable for British tax if you make 'substantial and habitual' visits to the UK, or if you have accommodation available for your use in the UK, however short the visit. This needs a little amplification.

Visits are regarded as 'substantial and habitual' if they average 90 days a year over four consecutive years. So you can spend up to 182 days in Britain in one year, as long as you counterbalance this with short visits in other years.

Accommodation 'available for your use' is interpreted as being a per-manent arrangement, whether or not you actually use the rooms. However, you can stay with members of your family, rent accommodation on a short-term basis, or retain a property (as long as it is let for a fixed period with no right of possession on your part), without infringing this stipulation. It does not apply to a person working full-time abroad.

ORDINARY RESIDENCE

The most important factor in connection with ordinary residence is that of continuity. The Inland Revenue interpret it as being the same as habitual residence. Shortly before leaving the UK you should obtain, complete, and forward to your usual Inspector of Taxes form P.85.

If you are going to be employed abroad for at least a complete tax year and you have a contract of service covering at least that period, then you are likely to be granted immediate non-resident and non-ordinarily resident status, together with any appropriate tax refund.

Employees who work overseas for at least 365 days, but less than a complete fiscal year, will not achieve non-ordinarily resident status, although the whole of their income will be exempt from UK tax, providing their visits to Britain do not exceed either 62 consecutive days or one-sixth of the total.

Employees who cannot meet the contract rule will probably have to complete a fiscal year working abroad before they are accepted as non-ordinarily resident. The waiting time is much more likely to be three tax years in the case of the self-employed and retired persons.

In all cases, providing the rules regarding visits and accommodation are not contravened, the status will be applied retrospectively to the date of leaving the UK, and any tax overpaid as a result will be refunded.

BRITISH TAX

Now, possibly after a long waiting period, you have at last attained non-resident and non-ordinarily resident tax status. This will exempt your overseas earnings, but most income arising in the UK will still be liable to British tax. (Remember that the Channel Islands and the Isle of Man are not part of the UK for tax purposes, as they have their own fiscal authorities which are quite independent.)

Some income arising in the UK is exempt from British tax, including income from certain Government stocks, state retirement pensions, plus interest on bank deposits and building society accounts. The latter is by concession only and cannot be obtained concurrently with a claim to partial UK allowances discussed below.

As a result of this, the expatriate should endeavour to transfer all assets out of the UK. There is no need to move them to Spain, which has strict exchange control regulations, but offshore investment is the ideal solution.

Pensions

Company and self-employed pensions are usually paid after deduction of the standard rate of British tax. Such non-ordinarily resident pensioners can apply to the Inspector of Foreign Dividends (Lynwood Road, Thames Ditton, Surrey) for payment gross or at a lower rate of deduction if it will be taxed in the country of residence. Pensions from Government sources are paid net of standard rate tax. If, as a result, you are suffering an excessively high tax deduction, you are able to claim partial UK tax allowances in roughly the same proportion as your UK taxable income bears to your total global income.

Capital gains tax avoidance

The timing of taking capital gains requires very careful planning, unless the liability is extinguished by exemptions and allowances. The main *exemptions* are on your private residence, possessions sold for less than £2000, and disposals of Government securities. The annual tax-free gains *allowance* is reviewed in each budget, and amounts to £6600 for 1987/88. In addition there may be business retirement relief or previous losses to offset.

If a balance remains which is subject to tax, then certainly attempt to delay taking the capital gain until you achieve non-ordinarily resident status, because it will then be exempt. 'How can I do that', you may ask, 'when I have to sell my business on a going concern basis?'. The solution (and one which you should take at the earliest possible stage to avoid it appearing like an artificial transaction to avoid the tax) is to incorporate your business as a limited company. Your financial adviser will tell you how such companies may be bought 'off the shelf' for as little as £100. You then retain the shares until you achieve the requisite tax status. In certain cases you may need to accept loan stock in exchange for shares. You should certainly take legal advice.

DOUBLE TAXATION TREATY

If you are not quite able to escape the British taxation net, then you have the advantage of the Double Taxation Treaty with Spain. Briefly it means that tax suffered in the country in which you are non-resident is offset against tax due in your country of residence. When your liability to Spanish tax has been calculated, if you have already paid that sum in British taxes then there is no further liability. However, if you have paid more tax in Britain than you are due to pay in Spain, this does not give entitlement to a refund.

The agreement specifies the following reduced rates of British tax deduction for British subjects resident in Spain:

▶ half the standard rate on dividends from British companies

▶ 12 per cent on interest arising in the UK

▶ 10 per cent on royalties arising in the UK

▶ nil on British annuities and occupational pensions

This is a valuable concession for authors, who are unlikely to be able to change their publisher in the way that others can alter their investments.

The Double Taxation Treaty is very welcome, because after you have been in Spain for 182 days in any calendar year, you will be liable for Spanish income tax, whether or not you have obtained a residence permit. This extends to the global income of both spouses, even if one is not resident in Spain at all.

Foreign owners letting property in Spain should be aware that they will be taxed in Spain on income exceeding 500,000 pesetas which arises in that country, even if they spend less than 182 days there in a calendar year.

SPANISH TAX

Income tax

Spanish income tax is called *renta,* and it rises on graduated scales from 8 per cent on a liability of 500,000 pesetas to 66 per cent on 12,200,000 pesetas, subject to an over-riding limit of 46 per cent of net taxable income. Remember that this is global income after allowable deductions, and you really should engage an *asesor fiscal* or a *gestor* to complete the tax returns, as they can save you money, even after paying their fees.

Tax is reduced by personal allowances, 30 per cent of the cost of purchase of a property in the first year only, or mortgage interest every year, plus life assurance and medical insurance premiums.

The annual tax return (of which there are two types, depending upon the size of your income) is generally due for completion in May or June for the preceding year. The relevant office is the *delegación de hacienda,* and the forms are obtained from the *estanco* (State tobacconist).

No tax return is required from persons with a global income of less than 500,000 pesetas per annum. Four per cent of the official value of your property is calculated as income each year.

Wealth tax

The so-called wealth tax *(patrimonio)* is levied (as far as residents are concerned) on global assets, which include all types of property, investments and bank balances. Mortgages and similar charges are deductable.

For residents there are personal allowances of 6 million pesetas for a single person, 9 million pesetas for a couple, and 750,000 pesetas for each child under eighteen years. Rates rise from 0.2 per cent on assets of up to 25 million pesetas to 2 per cent on 2.5 billion pesetas. Property is taken at its official value, which is often much less than its market value. Combined income and wealth tax assessments in any year are limited to a maximum of 70 per cent of taxable income.

Non-residents are liable for the tax on their assets in Spain, but they are not entitled to the personal allowances.

Inheritance tax

Although most Spanish taxes are lower than British ones, the exception is that Spanish inheritance tax starts at a much lower level and the rates can be higher, depending upon the relationship to the deceased person.

In Spain it is payable between spouses, which is not the case in Britain. It is assessed in Spain on property passing at death, irrespective of the residence or domicile of the deceased. Inheritances in favour of spouses, children or grandchildren are taxed at 3 per cent on the first 10,000 pesetas, rising to 21 per cent on the excess over 100 million pesetas.

As a rough guide to the approximate amount of inheritance tax payable on the average property found on the Costa Blanca, the first 3 million pesetas would attract 330,400 pesetas tax, with the marginal rate entering 13 per cent for the excess between 3 million and 10 million pesetas. Husbands can gamble by registering the property in the name of the wife, so that she would not pay inheritance tax in any event. Alternatively they could hedge their bets by registering in joint names, so that tax on half the value of the property would be payable by the survivor.

If there is liable to be any difficulty in meeting the tax, then the liability should be covered by life assurance, preferably of the first death policy type. Even better advice is to follow the suggestion in Chapter 9 to register the property in the name of your children, with the probability of avoiding the tax completely.

The rates for inheritances in favour of parents rise on the same scale from 5 per cent to 26 per cent. The gradations thereafter are very steep, depending upon the closeness of the relationship, until we reach the scale for unrelated beneficiaries which is from a minimum of 58 per cent on very small amounts up to a maximum of 84 per cent. The latter scale applies to common law spouses.

In all cases there is an additional tax where the legacy exceeds 10 million pesetas, being 7 to 10 per cent for spouses, children and grandchildren; 10 to 13 per cent for parents, and rising to 15 to 18 per cent for non-relatives.

Capital gains tax

There is a kind of capital gains tax in Spain which is levied on real estate and some investments. Although in theory it extends to global assets of residents, in practice this tax is not collected from foreigners on assets held outside Spain.

IVA

IVA (pronounced ee-vah), the Spanish equivalent of VAT, is currently set at 12 per cent on most items, and the system generally follows Common Market rules. The rate is 6 per cent on the purchase of a property and other items which are officially classified as 'basic necessities'. The rate is 33 per cent on 'luxury' goods, such as cars.

16

Investments

TAX EXEMPTION ON INTEREST

As pointed out in the previous chapter, interest on many British Government stocks held by overseas residents is exempted from UK taxation at source. However, it is still subject to Spanish income tax, and one of the features of the Double Taxation Agreement is that the countries concerned also exchange information!

Similarly, interest on building society and bank accounts may be exempted and paid gross to those not-ordinarily resident. However, this status may well take four years to achieve, which means that there could be a great deal of tax tied up to which you are unable to gain access. It is much better to close such accounts at the earliest possible stage, as they are not really suitable for non-residents.

National Savings Bonds are often a good investment for UK residents, although again the situation changes when you move abroad, and they lack stability of yield. They are also now subject to income tax.

OFFSHORE INVESTMENTS

There are various small tax havens around the world, and they have received this appellation because they are independent fiscal authorities which charge little or no tax. They pride themselves on confidentiality, as they do not and cannot be forced to give information to the British, Spanish, or any other tax authority.

Expatriates are placed in an exceptionally favourable tax position by purchasing shares in funds registered in such offshore places as the Channel Islands, Luxemburg, Hong Kong, Gibraltar, Bermuda, the Cayman Islands and the Netherlands Antilles; although some shareholders might have difficulty in finding their way to the latter if they wished to attend the Annual General Meeting of their company! In Jersey and Guernsey, for instance, income tax is about 20 per cent, but you only pay if you are resident on the island. Companies pay a fixed sum for Corporation Tax of £300, even if their profits amount to millions.

This does not mean that the offshore fund managers invest only in companies operating in the Channel Islands, Luxemburg or wherever; far from it. Various funds offer British Government stocks, besides a portfolio of shares in companies operating in the UK, Europe, North America, Australia, Japan and the Far East. In addition, there are funds specializing in commodities, bonds and currencies.

The various funds are rather like unit trusts to the extent that they spread the risk by investing as widely as possible. However, they differ because they are 'open-ended', or (as they are called in Luxemburg) variable capital companies: that is, the size of the fund can expand or contract as a result of buying and selling.

Another bonus is that your money is not tied up, as you can sell the whole or part of your shares at any time and receive the proceeds within a week or so.

These funds are quoted on the Stock Exchange and prices will be found listed daily in the *Financial Times* under the heading 'Offshore and Overseas'. You will see that in most cases two prices are quoted: the first is the 'bid' or price at which fund managers will buy back the shares from you; slightly higher by about 5 per cent is the 'offer' price, that is the selling price to you. The margin is to cover the costs of selling, advertising, registering your holding and the related work of paying dividends. Of course, it is rather like changing currencies - if you keep the same one then you do not get involved in this margin, and most people invest with long-term objectives. This margin, or charge, is called a 'front end load' in the market, and it may seem like a good idea to search for a fund where there is none.

In practice, such offshore funds seldom do well in terms of capital appreciation, as no one is promoting them.

GILTS

Gilts, or British Government stocks, are probably the safest form of investment, if you accept that the UK will never become bankrupt. That does not mean to say, though, that there is no risk at all. Like other stocks and shares, they can fall in price as well as rise, though they differ to the extent that they can fall in value only in the short term, as in the long term 'dated' stocks must be redeemed on or between specified dates by the British Government in accordance with the terms of the issue, such as £105 for each £100 of stock at maturity.

The 'mechanics' of gilts in simple terms are that they rise in price when other interest rates are falling, and vice versa. Generally there is a price change of about 10 per cent for every 1 per cent alteration in interest rate. Almost invariably they produce the highest level of income, although the return in terms of capital appreciation may be low. Beware of funds showing exceptionally high income, as this is often at the expense of a capital loss.

The most frequent interval for payment of interest is quarterly, although a monthly income can be obtained, if required, by investing in three separate funds with a spread of payment dates.

Many expatriates invest all their capital in gilts, but in doing so they overlook one important factor at their peril, and that is inflation. It is true that one of the advantages of gilts is that once you have bought them you are likely to continue to receive the same level of income, at least in the medium term, until the fund managers have to replace a stock which has matured. But what may seem like a comfortable level of income when you invest can easily be eroded by inflation and rising living costs to one which becomes insufficient. In that situation you are forced to sell off part of your capital in order to live, which further reduces your income, and you are on the first step of a downward spiral, which soon becomes a rollercoaster to penury. Another problem is that when your stock matures you may find it impossible to replace it with another stock that gives you an equivalent yield.

The best solution is to have part of your portfolio in equities (as shares in commercial companies are called), because over the years they have shown the ability to keep pace with and outstrip inflation. You could also consider switching to an offshore gilt fund, which offers the continuity of a portfolio of stocks, particularly if your stock is acceptable on favourable terms in full or part payment for the holding which you wish to acquire. As mentioned in the previous chapter, Spain does not operate a capital gains tax on these appreciations.

MANAGED FUNDS

For those of you with neither the inclination nor the (considerable) time necessary to become involved in the workings of the stock market, I would recommend managed funds. With this type of investment the fund managers switch from one market to another as current trends dictate. The 'front end load' is often just slightly higher than for other funds, although you are obtaining good value for this charge, as your investment is being actively managed on a continuing basis by experts with the most sophisticated communications technology equipment. In addition, you have two-tier security of risk spreading, because in effect your holding is like a unit trust investing in unit trusts.

Umbrella funds

Umbrella funds is a term much bandied around the markets, and this is a similar concept to the above for the more individually-minded investor who wants to make personal decisions. Managers with a large number of funds group them under one 'umbrella', and the investor has the option of switching from one to another for only a nominal fee.

Bond funds are a compromise between gilts and equities, as they often produce a moderately good income plus a fair degree of capital appreciation.

CURRENCY FUNDS

These are available in all the major world currencies but, due to the unpredictability of this investment, I would recommend them only for experts who know their way around the foreign exchange market. They can be useful in the short term as a retreat from equities when prospects for the latter are unfavourable.

Managed currency funds are available, although profits tend to be small as margins are narrow and contracting, due to governmental action to stabilize currencies.

PLANNING YOUR INVESTMENTS

Now that you know the different types of funds, you should decide upon your investment strategy. This will vary with every individual and there is no one right or wrong way. In my opinion you should approach the subject in the following manner.

When you are familiar with the cost of living and your probable annual expenses, decide how much income you need. From this figure deduct any income which you already have, such as one or more pensions; if a balance still remains, then invest the appropriate sum in gilt funds to produce the deficiency in income. Should gilts be falling rapidly in price (not yield) at that particular time, then delay your purchase until they stabilize by means of a holding operation in some alternative investment which is not likely to produce a short-term loss.

If you have still further funds to invest, then this should be done mainly for growth.

With sufficient confidence you can construct your own portfolio, which may contain a fair segment of international bond funds, on which you should receive an income of about 4 to 10 per cent, together with a fair capital appreciation. Beyond that the main limitation is your attitude to risk and your degree of sophistication in the investment market. Risk capital can earn extremely high rewards, sometimes over 200 per cent in a year, but even fund managers warn that such investments can be extemely volatile, and they should not form more than 10 per cent of your portfolio.

PROFESSIONAL ADVICE

Should you make use of the services of a financial adviser? My objective answer to that question (ignoring the bias that arises from the fact that I am one!) is strongly in the affirmative. The main point is that it will cost you nothing, as the financial adviser (like an insurance broker) is remunerated by commission from the fund managers. Do make certain, though, that this person is really independent, because if the so-called advisers represent only one fund or group, then whatever their qualifications or experience, they are and can be nothing but a salesman or woman. This is because they are retained by one organization, through salary or commission, to sell you one thing only, irrespective of whether it is the best, or indeed suitable for your needs. (In contrast, I, as an independant adviser, can offer my clients a choice of 200 of the best funds.)

A good financial adviser should have an appropriate professional qualification and the relevant experience. He/she will be able to give you both the long-term and the short-term record of each fund, besides being knowledgeable about the various markets and their prospects for the future. Many financial advisers also give their clients a great deal of helpful information on taxation without charge, although the commission in many cases does not cover their costs. Some will also charge only a percentage of the profit which they make for their clients, unlike portfolio managers who charge for fund-handling, whether or not a profit is made.

Should you have a minimum of about £20,000 to £30,000 for investment in other than purely gilt-edged stocks, then it is quite possible to obtain personal portfolio management – as distinct from the managed funds mentioned above. For this service most organizations take a percentage of the portfolio value, with a minimum stipulated charge. One disadvantage is that portfolio managers at a distance tend to act independently, particularly if communications are difficult, as on the Costa Blanca.

Besides the right qualifications and experience, a good portfolio manager also needs that indefinable flair for making a profit. Anyone can study past records, and note which stocks are rising and which falling; accurate prediction is another matter. The difficulty lies in the fact that stock markets move in cycles and depend mainly upon public confidence. There is a steady upward rise until people realize that a point of over-confidence has been reached, where the relationship of price to earnings no longer makes sense. So the next thing that is likely to happen with the fund which was rising so well and looked so safe is that its price drops sharply, and there is a correcting period of a year or two before it regains the price level at which you bought.

In contrast, a good financial adviser will give clients a choice (or a mixture) of funds which are about to make a large gain from a moderate position and others which have done badly in the past but are now in a recovery situation. The former produce a capital gain which averages around 65 per cent per annum, and the latter about 45 per cent. Naturally, there is less risk with the recovery funds, because you are buying cheaply and they are unlikely to fall much lower.

DIVIDENDS AND INTEREST

If desired, these can often be ploughed back or 'rolled up' to accumulate further shares. Should you wish to draw them, then it is a good idea to have them paid into a Channel Island or Gibraltar bank account, rather than direct to your Spanish bank account. There is no legal requirement to remit all your income to Spain.

RETURNS ON INVESTMENTS   MAY 1987

Investment	Interest/ dividend % p.a.	Capital appreciation % p.a.	Total return % p.a.
British banks			
Deposit	3.5	Nil	3.5
6 months fixed	6.4	Nil	6.4
High interest	6.0	Nil	6.0
Building societies			
Ordinary	5.0	Nil	5.0
High interest	6.7	Nil	6.7
3 months	7.7	Nil	7.7
National Savings			
Investment	10.0	Nil	10.0
Certificates	7.0	Nil	7.0
Bonds	12.2	Nil	12.2
Index certificates	4.0	4.0	8.0
Index bonds	8.0	4.0	12.0
Local Authority			
2 years	7.0	Nil	7.0
Money market			
3 months	6.7	Nil	6.7
Offshore funds			
Gilt-edged	12.6	10.8	23.4
UK equity	2.2	51.1	53.3
International equity	0.2	33.9	34.1
International managed	0.2	28.0	28.2
International bonds	5.8	17.6	23.4
North American	0.8	25.0	25.8
Australian	0.9	24.6	25.5
Japan	0.6	69.4	70.0
Far Eastern	0.8	44.2	45.0
Hong Kong	1.4	46.3	47.7
European	0.4	42.1	42.5
Commodity	1.0	16.3	17.3
Managed currency	5.3	21.7	27.0
Sterling currency	8.8	6.5	15.3
U.S. $ currency	5.9	7.2	13.1

WARNING Although the figures given for offshore funds are the mean per annum over a period of seven years for the average fund of the sector (the best performing fund can sometimes produce a total return as high as 290 per cent per annum), it should be appreciated that what has happened in the past is not necessarily a guide to probable events in the future. Independent professional financial advice should invariably be taken.

17
Insurances

HOUSE AND CONTENTS INSURANCE

The most valuable thing you own is likely to be your house, and you should be careful that it is fully covered at all times and that the cover is regularly reviewed in relation to escalating building costs.

If you are purchasing a property which has yet to be constructed, ask your solicitor to check at what stage you should commence insurance cover on the building, as the developer may be responsible until completion. Beware of the many developers who take out insurance cover for you at completion without telling you in advance, or asking you whether you want it. This is to ensure that they receive commission from the insurance company. Many new owners discover, too late, that they are dissatisfied with the cover provided, and they are stuck with it for a year until renewal date.

There is no reason why you should not ask the developer in advance whether he arranges cover and, if so, request details of the premium and the policy. Then you have time to shop around alternative companies before completion and decide which you prefer.

There is an inherent danger in one insurance company covering nearly all the properties in a locality, because if there is a disastrous flood, storm or fire, the massive claims could bankrupt the company.

Remember that the related contents may require separate cover, as your movable property could be in store, transit or temporary accommodation at different times.

You should be able to obtain a first-class policy underwritten at Lloyd's for a premium of £1.75 per £1,000 on buildings, and £6.25 per £1,000 on contents. Spanish premiums may be about 20 per cent less, but the exclusions are more wide ranging and there is a problem in obtaining payment of claims.

HEALTH INSURANCE

There is an enormous difference in cost between health insurance offered by British and Spanish companies. It is difficult to see why this should be so, unless either the British companies are making massive profits or the Spanish companies are setting premiums so low that their financial stability will be endangered. Here are a few British schemes which are open only to working expatriates. All premiums are the annual 1987 rates.

Europea Group
Cover £50,000 per person, except £1000 maternity and £500 dental.
Cost: single £250, married £365, each child £50.

Medicare
Cover unlimited, except £1000 maternity and home nursing 26 weeks.
Cost: single £288, married £576, family £779.

Some schemes are restricted to persons under the age of 65 such as:

BUPA
Cover £50,000, except nil for maternity, home nursing, G.P. and dental plus self-induced sickness.
Cost: under 50 £255; 50-64 £380; child £85.
Evacuation £66, child £22.

The only British scheme accepting the 65 to 75 age group which I have found is:

Exeter Hospital Aid Society
Cover variable according to scales and units.
Cost for middle range: under 65, single £266, married £373.

There is a one-time-only extra joining premium for the over 65's varying from .25 to 4.5 times the norm according to age.

Turning now to Spanish schemes, of which there are hundreds, the sheer proliferation shows that, however good the state medical service is, Spaniards find it desirable, if not essential, to take out private health insurance. Most differ from British schemes in that they are restricted to a local area (although often extendable without extra charge). Few cover traffic and work accidents. To give one typical example:

Unión Previsora (UPSA)
All costs paid by a booklet of 'cheques'.
Exclusions are pre-existing illnesses, all accidents, together with op-

erations within 6 months of joining, unless certified by a doctor as urgent.
Cost: under 60 £108; 60-69 £150; 70-79 £180.

Entitlement to treatment by the British National Health Service will cease when you become a resident in Spain, except for emergencies which occur during a visit to Britain. If you are in receipt of a British retirement or widow's pension, then you can join the Spanish National Health Service by completing form UK/E17, obtained from the DHSS, Overseas Group, Newcastle upon Tyne, NE98 IYX. The form should be taken to your nearest Social Security office in Spain.

Retired readers will decide for themselves whether they find the service adequate for their needs. It does not cover convalescence, extended or geriatric nursing. One of the main problems encountered is that few of the doctors speak much English or other foreign languages.

VEHICLE INSURANCE

It is advisable to shop around in advance of your need, as premiums can vary by more than 60 per cent between different companies. One of the cheapest which I have found is Apolo of Alfonso X el Sabio 34, Alicante, telephone 520 03 74. For third-party cover they charge about £75 for a small car, rising to around £100 for a moderately-powerful vehicle.

Third party is the only insurance which is compulsory for drivers, and only a very small proportion take out more comprehensive cover. Perhaps the reasons are the high cost, the difficulty of obtaining payment for claims, and the fact that relatively few cars are stolen, although you should expect a break-in if you install a radio or leave valuables on view.

TRAVEL INSURANCE

Many people take out travel insurance for isolated journeys through the agency arranging the tickets. This is probably not the most economic method for   someone who makes a large number of trips annually between different countries; such a traveller should consult an insurance broker regarding which multi-trip policy is most suited to his/her needs.

LIFE ASSURANCE

Life assurance is something for which I normally have little regard. In Spain, however, it is desirable because it helps meet the heavy liability of inheritance tax; there is also the added bonus that the premiums may be deducted from Spanish income tax due.

It is well worth considering an offshore single premium life assurance bond, as this can be a very profitable investment, even excepting the above advantages.

Funerals are very expensive in Spain, and if you wish to take out insurance cover of £500 for this purpose, it will cost you annually about £39 at age 50, £53 at 60 and £89 at 70.

18
Banking

One of the most important considerations when selecting a bank in Spain is that of language. It could be the best bank in town, but if you are not fairly fluent in Spanish and cannot make yourself understood, then it may not be a lot of help to you. So try to find a bank where at least two of the relatively senior staff speak a language which you understand.

Another important point is waiting time. If your choice falls on a bank in one of the most popular areas for tourists, there may be long delays in obtaining service, particularly during the busy season. From the customer's point of view, there is no difference between the so-called savings banks *(Cajas de Ahorros)* and other banks as they both provide identical services.

TYPES OF ACCOUNT

A non-resident, or a new arrival who has not yet obtained a *residencia,* may wish to open both a convertible peseta account and an ordinary peseta account. The former is desirable to pay for the purchase of property, unless you are paying the seller directly and are absolutely certain that a foreign money contribution will be recorded. Ordinary (i.e. non-convertible) pesetas cannot be paid into a convertible peseta account.

Within both types of accounts you may have one or more of a current, a savings and/or a fixed period deposit account.

With a *current* account you obviously have a cheque book, and the account earns a very small amount of interest on the balance, typically 0.1 per cent per annum.

With a *savings* account you can pay in or draw out money at any time and earn about 1 per cent per year interest, although you will not have a cheque book.

With a minimum sum of 100,000 pesetas you may open a *fixed period deposit* account for 3,6 or 12 months, typically earning from 6 to 10 per cent per annum, depending upon current money market conditions, the length of the term and the size of the deposit. The interest rate is fixed initially and it is invariable. For residents only 15 per cent is withheld against possible income tax liability. Remember to deduct this on your annual tax return from the amount of tax owing.

In the event of need, the deposit may be withdrawn before maturity with loss of part or all of the interest or even a penalty, depending upon the exact stage in the term when withdrawal takes place.

Non-residents may also, if they wish, open one or more foreign currency accounts operated in selected foreign currencies. This type of account may be opened with a bank draft from another country or a personal cheque drawn on an overseas bank, but not with foreign currency notes. A foreign currency account earns a rate of interest which fluctuates constantly depending upon international money market conditions.

Once you obtain your *residencia* you are permitted to operate only an ordinary peseta account. Permanent residents are liable to incur penalties if they operate any other type of account, as they are contravening the exchange control regulations and breaking the law.

Unless they are buying property, tourists will not normally open a bank account in Spain, as they can exchange travellers' cheques, Eurocheques up to 25,000 pesetas for each cheque, and foreign currency notes at most banks. If they wish to keep commission charges to a minimum then they will obtain travellers' cheques expressed in pesetas.

USING A SPANISH BANK ACCOUNT

Now here are a few point about operating a Spanish bank account. The first, which may come as a surprise to you, is that foreign personal cheques take about one month to clear. Consequently, if you have various expenses to meet at completion of the property which you are buying, or furniture to purchase locally, then it is advisable to bring sufficient travellers' cheques or Eurocheques with you when you travel to Spain.

When writing cheques in Spain it is usual to put the sign for numbered (#) before and after the amount in figures to prevent alteration. Most banks will accept the amount in words written in English if you do not know Spanish. When the payee is shown as *portador* this strictly translates to 'bearer', although it is also used when drawing cash from your own account.

FOREIGN CURRENCIES

A permanent resident can only transfer limited amounts of money outside of Spain. As there is no legal requirement to remit the whole of your income to Spain (up to half of your salary may go to another country if you are employed; 65% if you are non-resident), it is useful to have funds available in other countries, should the need arise for additional foreign exchange or to make investments abroad. The amount of foreign currency which a resident may obtain at present is limited to the following:

▶ for trips abroad, up to the equivalent of 350,000 pesetas per person per journey

▶ for hospital fees and medical expenses contracted abroad, no limit

▶ the actual cost of students' fees, expenses and incidentals without limit

▶ small transfers of up to 50,000 pesetas each month without the necessity of official permission

Non-residents may carry up to a maximum of 100,000 pesetas per person in cash when leaving Spain. They may change up to 500,000 pesetas, provided they can prove (by means of exchange vouchers) that they have brought that amount of money into Spain.

19
Legal matters

When selecting a Spanish solicitor, your must again bear in mind any possible language difficulties (as well as the general level of charges to be expected). Probably you will be guided on both matters by the conversations you have with local friends and acquaintances, besides their recommendations.

Some matters might be dealt with quite adequately and at lower cost by a *gestor* (pronounced hes-TOR). The latter has no exact equivalent outside of Spain, although the nearest counterpart would probably be a legal executive, except that he is self-employed and not on the staff of a solicitor. However, satisfy yourself that the *gestor* is legally qualified and not a 'cowboy' Mr Fixit with a smattering of foreign languages. For those people who do not speak Spanish and feel frustrated by a wall of bureaucracy, a *gestor* can cut a way through to obtain residence permits, work permits, driving licences, car transfers and registrations, besides dealing with tax returns and even wills.

WILLS

Spanish

Every expatriate who has property in Spain should make a Spanish will covering the assets in Spain. The main reason is that the expenses involved in distributing the estate to the beneficiaries is considerably higher when there is only a foreign will or no will at all. There should be a further will made in the persons' home country covering assets elsewhere in the world than Spain.

The procedure for making a will in Spain is to go to a solicitor or a reliable *gestor* and tell him how you wish to dispose of your estate. Remember that under Spanish law you have no choice on how one-third of your estate is distributed, limited discretion on another third, and complete freedom regarding the remaining third. This is the Spanish law of obligatory heirs, whereby one-third goes in equal shares to children (or their children or grandchildren); another third is temporarily a life interest for a spouse; (though if there is none, or at the death of the spouse, it goes to children and their issue as you select and in the proportions which you decide), and the remaining third can be left to whomever you wish.

Should you desire to leave a legacy of any kind to a distant relative or someone completely unrelated (which includes a common-law spouse in the eyes of the Spanish law), it is preferable to do so from your will made in another country, as inheritance tax rates in Spain vary according to the closeness of the blood relationship, and the highest rate of between 58 and 84 per cent applies to non-relatives, depending upon the value of the bequest.

Having instructed your legal representative, you will then be called upon by a *notario* (chosen by your representative) to sign the will in the presence of witnesses. The original will is retained by the *notario*, who sends details to the Registro Central de Ultima Voluntad in Madrid. If you wish, you can have made an ordinary copy or an authenticated one of the will.

There are simple forms of 'home-made' wills, but they are likely to cause more expense than they save, especially if you contravene the law of obligatory heirs.

British

In addition, you should make a will in your home country, though it may not be necessary to travel there for this purpose, as English law permits such a will to be signed and witnessed in Spain. This will should give the disposal of all assets outside of Spain.

Where you keep your assets, other than immovable ones such as real estate, will probably depend upon your liability for inheritance taxes, and the Spanish ones are fully detailed in Chapter 15. The main difference in Britain is that inheritance tax is not charged between spouses; to others the first £90,000 is free of tax, the next £50,000 is charged at 30 per cent, the next £80,000 at 40 per cent, the next £110,000 at 50 per cent, and any excess at 60 per cent. You will have read in the chapter on taxation that it is domicile, as interpreted by the Inland Revenue authorities, which decides liability for British inheritance tax, and that this is not necessarily where you live or keep your assets.

ABSENTEE OWNERS

Absentee owners should remember that they are under a legal liability to appoint a Spanish resident to deal with matters such as rates and taxes in their absence. You may decide to entrust such details to a solicitor, *gestor*, bank, friend, or any other person who is legally resident.

It is advisable to have someone nearby keeping an eye on your property in case an insurance claim is necessary for damage caused by fire, flood or storm, as this has to be submitted within a limited interval under the terms of most policies. Do not necessarily rely on property developers to inform you, as they may have very close links with the insurance company which will have to pay the claim.

BIRTHS, MARRIAGES AND DEATHS

Whistling through a lifetime, let us start with births. However short your stay, or whatever your nationality, these must be registered in Spain. Either parent should take the certificate received from the doctor or matron to the local *ayuntamiento* and obtain a *certificado literal de nacimiento*. The latter should then be taken, together with both parents' birth certificates and their marriage certificate, plus the father's passport, to the parents' consulate for registration. Baptism can be arranged in Spain, if desired, according to faith.

A church wedding is only possible in Spain if at least one of the parties is a Roman Catholic. A minimum of three weeks notice will be required. If one party only is a Roman Catholic, then it may take longer, as the Spanish church authorities have to give special permission.

Where both parties are Roman Catholics, the documents required will be certificates from their previous priests that they are of that faith and free to marry, baptismal certificates, and consent of the parents in writing where either is under age.

Those who are not Roman Catholics can only be married at the Civil Registry. This can be followed, if desired, by a church ceremony which is not recognized as a marriage. Whatever the faiths, if either party has had a foreign divorce, then a solicitor will probably be needed to deal with the required formalities.

British and American citizens can marry at a registry in Gibraltar. Firstly, one of them should visit their consulate in Spain, and arrange for the necessary form to be completed. This should then be sent to the Registrar of Marriages, 30b, Town Range, Gibraltar, accompanied by the fee, and a special licence is usually available in a few days. Two witnesses to the ceremony will be required, as well as the passports of the parties being married.

If divorce is contemplated then, as in any other country, the aggrieved party should consult a solicitor. The usual grounds for divorce are accepted in Spain, such as cruelty, desertion and adultery. Generally, the parties have to live apart for at least a year before a divorce can be granted by a judge specializing in family law. The latter will give judgement on maintenance, shares of common property, and custody of children, in the absence of voluntary agreement on these matters.

Finally, death should be registered at the *ayuntamiento* by someone who knew the deceased. A doctor's certificate giving the cause of death will be required, and a Spanish death certificate will be issued. This needs to be taken to the deceased person's consulate, who will issue a death certificate valid in the home country. As an alternative to an expensive burial, persons may be able to make advance arrangements with a local hospital to donate their body to medical science.

Regarding the distribution of the estate in Spain, this is a matter for a Spanish solicitor, however small it may be and even if everything is to pass to the surviving spouse. The reason is that inheritance tax is due in any case and must be paid within six months of death. If there is a Spanish will, these matters are considerably simplified. Should there be a foreign will only, it will be acted upon after probate has been obtained and legalized. In cases where the person died intestate, the distribution will be to relations as stated in the Spanish law of obligatory heirs.

20
Community life

The advantages of having neighbours of the same nationality and/or language as your own include the ease of communication, sharing a common culture, social contacts within a known and established framework, mutual assistance in dealing with problems and sharing tasks, similarity of interests, passing of information, and generally easing the culture shock of settling into a foreign country by limited exposure. These are quite considerable and certainly not to be discounted. Even so, there are some disadvantages, particularly in regard to the 'colonial' mentality and outlook, the negative approach of spending one's time denigrating Spaniards and all their institutions. If you have few Spanish neighbours this may make you lazy concerning the learning of their language and culture, which results in only partial acceptance of your new home.

For an outline of how community life should be organized, we have to consider the relevant laws–the Ley de Propiedad Horizontal for connected properties, and the Entidad Urbanística Colaboradora de Conservación y Gestíon for detached villas. These laws apply whether a block of flats or a massive urbanization the size of a town is concerned, the important point being that there is some element of shared ownership.

But the law provides only the framework; the details of how a community is run are left to the owners. Therefore, you have only yourself to blame if you do not like the rules, should you have neglected to attend the meetings or to vote. Absent owners are entitled to appoint a proxy to attend and vote for them and the proxy does not need to be an owner.

At the first annual general meeting the rules of the community are drawn up, the officers are elected, a budget is agreed and the contribution from owners is approved. The rules must state whether each owner has an equal share in the common property and, if not, how the shares are calculated. This decides the respective voting rights and the share of the contribution to community expenses. There is no reason why you should not ask to see the regulations of a community where you are considering buying a property. Without a unanimous vote of all the owners it is very difficult to have them changed.

Subsequent annual general meetings will appoint replacements for any officers, if necessary, consider the previous year's accounts, besides dealing with the same matters as at the first meeting. Points which owners should be on their guard against at such meetings are approving the election of officers for exceptionally long periods (one third of the committee to retire each year, decided by ballot, would be ideal) and the sanctioning of excessive interference in the private property of owners, as this is not the true function of the committee, which is there mainly to deal with common property. Owners with a total of at least a quarter of the voting rights may call a general meeting.

The only official required by law to be elected is the *presidente*, and he must be an owner. In addition there may be, if desired, an administrator, a secretary, or a treasurer; they may be paid and they do not need to be owners. These officers (which means the *presidente* if there are no others) are responsible for the running and maintenance of community services, keeping community property in a good state of repair, formulating the budget, collecting urbanization charges from owners, keeping the minutes of meetings and dealing with other matters approved by the owners in general meetings. Such officials find that they are often kept quite busy on a large development.

Many communities with multi-national ownership find that they have difficulty in dealing with business at general meetings. Almost invariably this is due to language problems, which could be avoided by organization, planning and forethought. Some spend many hours verbally translating the minutes of the previous meeting. This is totally unnecessary and a waste of owners' time. The secretary (or *presidente* if there is none) should arrange for the notice of the meeting, together with the previous minutes and any information to be voted on, to be distributed in advance in a language which each owner understands, as far as possible. The minutes can then be taken as read, and the task of voting on resolutions is simplified considerably if owners have a prior understanding of the facts.

If you are looking to the community to provide the lead and the crystalization for a busy social life and a range of activities, then it is your responsibility to select and vote for committee members who are like-minded and who are prepared to work to develop these facilities. It is very difficult for a private owner to do so if the committee is unhelpful or opposed to such progress.

21
Learning Spanish

If you are contemplating going to live in Spain in the future, the time is never too soon to start learning Spanish. It is a very useful language, spoken in over a dozen countries, and also one of the easiest to learn. Many of the words are the same or very similar to English. So begin to learn it in your own country at the earliest possible stage; even five years before you move to Spain is not too soon, provided that you make use of the language on occasions.

TUITION IN ENGLAND

You may well find that facilities for learning Spanish are better in your own country than in Spain. There may be evening classes near to where you live; some polytechnics run intensive courses when other students are on vacation, and there are also the commercial language schools. Your local reference library will be able to tell you about the possibilities.

TUITION IN SPAIN

Once you arrive in Spain you may find that there is very little choice. There are a few commercial language schools on the Costa Blanca, particularly to the north of Alicante. It is pointless for me to make comparisons between them, as you will obviously not travel a distance to classes. The one that is convenient to where you live will be either acceptable or not. You will find their advertisements in the local newspapers. The main point to watch for is the size of the classes, as your progress is likely to be in inverse ratio to the number of students.

To ensure that you achieve a good and accurate accent, have as your teacher a native Spanish speaker, as a foreigner can, at best, give only an approximate rendition of the pronunciation.

AUDIO-VISUAL

A third alternative is the audio-visual method of learning, which I consider by far the best, as the eye is far more retentive than the ear. In the normal classroom method your teacher would probably be very pleased if you remembered half of the vocabulary until the next lesson. I have found that the audio-visual method typically gives about 97 per cent retention for at least three months, and, after all, retention is what it is all about. It is no use learning the words one day and forgetting them the next.

PRIVATE TUITION

Private tuition may be possible if a language school is not convenient. Do not expect it to be cheap: one-to-one instruction means that you will have to pay a full economic hourly rate. Possibly you may have friends prepared to make up a small class, and so reduce the cost per student. With this method, insist on a planned programme of instruction and make regular checks on your own progress, otherwise your teacher may make it a job for life!

BOOKS AND CASSETTES

Self-instruction may be perfectly possible, but try not to do this solely from a book which gives no pronunciation. If you learn to pronounce incorrectly by Anglicizing the words, you will find it much harder to cure your bad accent in the future than you did learning it in the first place! So the combination of cassette and book is far better than only the latter. You may find a set available on loan from your public library before you leave home.

MUTUAL TEACHING

Many Spaniards want to learn English, or some other language. You can turn this to your mutual advantage at no cost by offering to teach one another your own language. This works best if both students are at approximately the same level, whether it is beginner, intermediate or advanced.

Similarity of age group or interests is an added bonus, although this is not essential. Probably the way that this form of learning is best organized is in a series of dialogues on various topics, which are given in one language and then repeated in the other.

REGIONAL VARIATIONS

Spain does not have just one language, and Spanish does not have an invariable pronunciation. Throughout most of Spain the people speak what is known as Castellano, the Spanish which originated in the province of Castile.

Particularly along the Costa Brava and in the Balearic Islands, Catalan is spoken, which is a separate language and not a dialect.

Around the Pyrenees and near the north coast they speak Basque, which again is a separate language.

In the Costa Blanca region the Alicantino and Valenciano dialects still survive. Children in the area have the option of going to a school where they are taught. You may see them on bi-lingual signposts and a few official forms. However, there is really no point in a foreigner learning Alicantino or Valenciano, unless it is for a special reason such as an author conducting historical research.

In Andalucia, in the south of Spain, together with the Canary Islands and the whole of Hispanic Latin-America, a slightly different pronunciation is found. Castellano has the distinctive 'th' sound for the letter 'z', and also for 'c' when it precedes 'e' or 'i'. The other regions mentioned pronounce these sounds as an 's'. You will never be considered as pronouncing incorrectly if you stick to the Castellano form, although in Latin-America it is regarded as effeminate!

Do learn Spanish in a systematic way. Those who say they will 'pick it up as they go along' seldom reach the stage of being able to string even a simple sentence together.

22
Education

CHILDREN IN SPAIN

Younger residents with children will have to consider their education. If the children are living with them in Spain, there is a legal requirement to send them to school from the age of six until they reach fifteen.

Privately-run kindergartens take small children from about the age of two years. For the very young language is never a problem; they will learn Spanish the natural way, as we learn our own language - by listening and repeating.

Older children will obviously have a considerable problem in a state school, because at first they will hardly understand a word of the instruction, and it will be some time before they become fluent enough to follow the lessons.

Personally, I am not in favour of intensive language courses for children, as they are so very exhausting mentally. Consequently, parents with children coming to live on the Costa Blanca should give this matter careful thought in relation to the place in which they decide to live, as private schools giving instruction in English and a British education are extremely few and they are mostly day schools only. Apart from kindergartens there are really only two main choices.

Undoubtedly the better, as its curriculum extends to advanced level, is the Sierra Bernia School at La Cañeta, San Rafael, Alfaz del Pi, which is 8km (5 miles) north of Benidorm. The school was established in 1973 and has about 120 pupils between the ages of four and eighteen. It is a day school. The headmaster, Duncan M. Allan, can be telephoned on (965) 588-9449.

Rather newer and (unusually for Spain) quite well equipped for science subjects with a laboratory is the St. Andrews International College at Partida de Sanz, Benidorm. It takes both day and boarding pupils, preparing them for the GCSE examinations. The school offers a wide range of sports facilities. The telephone number of the head teacher, Mrs Ann Birch, is (965) 585-5863.

CHILDREN IN ENGLAND

Because of the difficulties mentioned above, you may decide to leave your children with relatives, or send them to a private or public school in your home country. Unless you have personal knowledge of a particular school then the choice can be quite daunting. There are two organizations in Britain which can be of considerable assistance in this respect. Both are educational advisory services for independent schools. They are Gabbitas-Thring, 6 Sackville Street, Piccadilly, London, W1X 2BR (tel. 01-7340161) and Truman & Knightley Educational Trust Ltd, 78 Notting Hill Gate, London, W11 (tel. 01-7271242). As both are charitable trusts they offer consultations free of charge. They prefer parents to see them in person, but if this is not possible than they will give advice by letter or telephone.

The Independent Schools Information Service (ISIS) at 56 Buckingham Gate, London, SW1 6AG (tel: 01-6308793) produces comprehensive regional guides to most of the independent schools in Britain.

ADULT EDUCATION

With considerable time to spare in Spain, some adults may wish to extend their education. Little assistance in this regard can be obtained from the state authorities, as there is little adult education available for ever their own nationals, and you would need to be fairly fluent in Spanish to gain some benefit.

Many people overlook the possibility of following educational, technical or hobby subjects by correspondence course. This method is used extensively in large countries with communication problems, such as Brazil, the USSR and the USA.

It is a matter on which I can write with a little authority, as, besides being the first Secretary of the Correspondence Colleges Standards Association, I have been author, editor and tutor of a number of commercial courses, and taught students of various nationalities from all over the world. There were many success stories, and the main reason for any failures was generally lack of motivation.

The educational trusts mentioned above will advise on these courses without charge, as they receive commission, although I have not found them particularly knowledgeable regarding correspondence colleges.

If you wish to follow an Open University course, then you will need to consult with the admissions office at Milton Keynes at a very early stage, regarding whether you can obtain the related broadcasts by radio and satellite television, besides attending vacation courses in the UK.

Morning typing courses are available at St. Andrews International College, mentioned above, for adults and school leavers.

CULTURAL EDUCATION

Spanish culture is very rich, and your efforts to appreciate it will be repaid in full measure. Obviously the first step is to learn the language before you can study it in detail, although there are some books in English and other languages.

To see the best of Spain's cultural heritage you will need to travel a little further afield from the Costa Blanca to Granada, Seville, Córdoba, Toledo, Segovia, and Burgos, amongst other places. Even the Costa Blanca, though, can offer interesting castles - not only the Castillo de Santa Barbara in Alicante, which can be ascended by lift from the beach, but also in the countryside around if you like to make a circuit of Novelda (for Mola), Sax, Villena, Biar, Albaida, Guadalest and Polop, near to La Nucia. Many of them are in a very good state of preservation and they are often ignored by tourists and residents alike.

BOOKS

English books and others in different languages are not easy to buy in the area, so it is advisable to take a supply with you, if possible. You will find a small stock in the department store Galerias in Alicante, besides some of the larger *librerías*. Advertisements can be seen in the local papers for secondhand books. In addition, small libraries are sometimes kept at various international and British clubs.

For a much wider choice, the larger bookstores in your home country will always send you books by post. This need not prove too expensive if you circulate them around a group of friends with similar reading tastes.

Generally, there is no difficulty in obtaining the popular newspapers of most of the major European countries within one or two days. Magazines are probably best obtained by subscription if you are concerned about continuity of supply.

23

Shopping

DEPARTMENT STORES

Department stores in the area are few and far between. Centrally situated in Alicante, on the corner of the Avenidas de Maissonave and Federico Soto (with underground parking approached from the rear) is *Galerias Preciados*. There is a wide selection of goods on four floors, plus a cafeteria. A 10 per cent discount is available if you bring your passport. Their prices seem very reasonable.

At the time of writing, land has just been obtained in Alicante to build a branch of *El Corte Inglés,* probably the best-known department store in the cities of Spain. A branch is operating in Murcia, which is reasonably convenient to residents in the Torrevieja area with their own transport, besides which there is a frequent railway service between Alicante and Murcia. There is another branch in Valencia.

HYPERMARKETS

Hypermarkets with good parking space can be found, such as *Pryca* on the outskirts of Alicante, alongside the road to San Vicente Raspeig, and other branches to the north-east. The only hypermarket convenient to residents in the southern part of the Costa Blanca is *Continente* near Elche, about 4 km (2½ miles) along the road towards Crevillente. Considerable savings can be made on the wide range of goods in this very extensive store.

MARKETS

Most of the larger towns in the area have permanent covered markets where you can buy vegetables, fruit, meats, fish, cheese, and a variety of other produce. Do not expect to haggle, as prices are fixed. Neither should you assume that prices will be low, particularly during the tourist season; you can often buy cheaper at shops in the residential areas populated mainly by Spaniards. I always look for a stall or shop where I can take a bag and select exactly what I want; in this way a proportion of poor quality or deteriorating produce is avoided.

Some stallholders are 'short change artists'; first they give you the coins, pause, then the small notes, finally the large notes. There is a long interval between each stage, when they hope that you will walk away, assuming that you have been given all your change. So be familiar with the currency and how much your bill totals, otherwise it can prove to be a very expensive market for you!

Weekly markets in the open air are held as follows:

Monday	Callosa de Ensarria
	Denia
	La Nucia
	Santa Pola
Tuesday	Altea
Wednesday	Benidorm
	Benitachell
	Campello
	Ondara
	Petrel
	Teulada
	Guardamar
Thursday	Jávea
	Villajoyosa
	Alicante
Friday	Alfaz del Pi
	Finestrat
	Gata de Gorgos
	La Nucia
	Moraira
	Torrevieja
Saturday	Benisa
	Calpe
	Alicante
Sunday	Benidorm

Please be warned that pickpockets are very active and extremely skilled, particularly in those markets frequented by tourists; so make certain that your money and valuables are quite safe.

Whilst vegetables and fruit will almost certainly be cheaper than you can buy elsewhere, this is not necessarily the case with other items; I have seen many things priced well above the level in a big department store in Alicante, even though overheads are much higher for the latter. So know the local prices in advance for the items which you want to buy.

Most traders strongly resent efforts to bargain, possibly fearing the setting of a precedent. However, there is no reason why you should not ask for a quantity discount if you are buying more than one item.

Wherever you buy clothing in Spain the price is likely to be considerably higher than in Britain, particularly for cotton items, even though this crop is grown on the Costa Blanca! Consequently, it is advisable to stock up before you leave home. There is the additional problem that styles and cuts may not be to your taste in Spain. Leather items and shoes are a good buy locally. Similarly, men's made to measure and off the peg lightweight suits compare very favourably in price with northern European tailors.

24
Gardening

Before you begin to plant a single item, whether your garden is large or small, the first thing you should do is plan how you expect your garden to look when it is established. Too many people plant odd bits and pieces at different times, so that the result is a hotchpotch. When planning the interior decoration of your home, you consider such matters as theme, colour and balance; similar thought should be given to your garden, which provides the exterior decoration.

Since, unlike houses, gardens are not covered, there are the additional factors presented by the elements to consider. Probably the most important of these is sun and shade. Almost anything will grow if it has sufficient water, but many plants cannot tolerate the hot sunlight for most of the day; consequently, such plants need the shade of a southern wall, trees or bushes. So in your planning, notice where the shadows fall and locate your dependent areas accordingly. In some areas, strong winds may need to be taken into consideration.

Besides sun and shade we also need to consider the seasons. The Costa Blanca has a long hot dry summer. There may be few clouds and no rain for months at a time. If you are able to delay your planting until the late autumn, then this will give your young plants a much better chance to become established, rather than being shrivelled in the summer heat. In any case, rainwater is very much better for them than tap water with its chemical additives.

It is also important to consider the flowering seasons of various plants to give you a display of colour throughout the year. So at the earliest opportunity take notice of other people's gardens as you walk along the pavements, as these will present ideas and highlight the mistakes. For instance, you will see the various oleanders produce flowers throughout the summer, and the geraniums have a very long flowering season. Bougainvillaea is a good climber with a little assistance, and it throws a riot of blooms around an arch.

Lawns are not my recommendation, unless you have plenty of large shade trees as protection from the scorching effect of the sun's rays. On the Costa Blanca it is very rare to see a good lawn. They almost invariably entail the use of a sprinkler system for many hours every day to prevent a shrivelled appearance. This leads to three problems: water pressure may be so low as to prevent proper operation of a sprinkler; the use for this purpose may be banned for long periods during drought conditions, and water is metered with a charge levied according to usage.

Gravel is therefore widely used to cover areas which are not planted. It can give a satisfactory appearance if the gravel is the right size and colour (through note that white gravel causes visual discomfort), and the area covered forms a reasonable balance within the garden as a whole. The most frequent mistake made with the use of gravel is to use it to cover far too extensive an area. It has obvious advantages for assisting drainage of at times heavy rainfall.

Natural top soil is almost invariably thin, poor in nutrients and lacking in humus. This dries out very quickly and fails to hold the water for long, even when there is rain. Consequently, if you have a fair sized garden, you will need to purchase one or more loads of top soil. If you can obtain it from an alluvial river basin, then this is likely to be the most fertile.

For smaller areas, and for planting items which require special treatment, it is best to buy a bag of peat or compost. Horse or animal manure is not advisable for gardens, as it tends to attract too many insects to the area. Volcanic soil is well adapted to extracting the humidity out of the night air, even in summer; consequently, its use is recommended around areas which have lakes or *salinas*.

Drought-resistant plants certainly make the gardener's work easier and they are well worth selecting. They can often be recognized by their fleshy leaves and stems. Restrict their area or they may grow to weed proportions.

Varied cacti can make an interesting display in a corner of your garden. Young spiky-leaved agave cacti can be dug up on the sand dunes, but remember that they grow to a massive size, throwing up a great seed head after about seven years, before dying as a result of this effort. Their roots are a favourite hiding place for snakes! (Note, too, that loose rubble is not a good thing to have in your garden as it is beloved by scorpions).

There is no reason why you should avoid growing vegetables. Even though market prices may be fairly cheap, the produce deteriorates rapidly in handling during the hot weather, and it is so much nicer picked freshly from your own garden. I cannot understand why so many people use nearly all their vegetable garden to grow potatoes, since these are one of the cheapest vegetables and deteriorate least in transit. So choose the vegetables that you like and find a little expensive, as long as the cultivation is not beyond your capabilities. Remember that peas are a very beneficial crop because they put nitrogen into the soil.

Another decision which amazes me is that most people select purely decorative trees in preference to useful ones. Personally, I am a firm believer in planting fruits and nuts, which can be attractive as well as useful. Oranges, lemons, peaches and almonds, besides many others, grow particularly well in the region, and young trees can be bought very cheaply. Vines can be trained over trelliswork to improve the appearance of a property and produce fruit for dessert.

25
Pastimes and sports

TELEVISION

Television tends to occupy much less of the spare time of most expatriates in Spain compared to when they lived in Britain, even though they have more leisure time available. The main reason is that imported sets suitable for channels in northern Europe have to be converted to receive Spanish television stations. The latter are of very limited interest to expatriates who cannot speak the language, except for sport (and even then only when it is international) and musical programmes. Satellite television overcomes some of these problems by providing up to 12 programmes in different languages, with probably two or three in English.

There are also the installation charges on an urbanization to bear in mind, and these are likely to amount to at least £325, plus £5 per month for maintenance. A suitable colour set with facility for 12 channels should be available for around £200 in the large hypermarkets or department stores. No licence is required. Television programmes are listed in the local newspapers.

RADIO

Radios with only long and medium wave bands have similar limitations. There are hopes of a one hour broadcast in English from a local station. Failing that, you may have to pick up Radio Algiers for the news in English! For reception of northern European stations you will need a radio with two or three short wave bands, preferably from 5 up to 16 MHz. In Spain this is likely to cost you about £40 to £50, and it is better to buy a Russian-made set for half this cost before you leave Britain.

Details of the BBC's World Service programmes appear in a fair amount of detail in the local English press. The best reception is on 5.975 MHz (50.21 mts.) and 15.07 MHz (18.91 mts.). A recommended radio selling for 6,145 pesetas in some local hypermarkets is the Philips D-2225, which has five wavebands including two shortwave.

READING

The availability of books and publications in English and other languages has been discussed in Chapter 22. As you become more proficient at Spanish you really should attempt to read newspapers and periodicals in that language; this will not only expand your vocabulary, but also increase your confidence, so that you soon find that you can follow complete articles with little difficulty.

GAMES

To complete some of the indoor pastimes, such games as whist, bridge and chess are very popular everywhere and you will almost certainly find clubs organizing such tournaments in most places with a fair population. Bingo is also a regular favourite, as well as dancing of all kinds, the commercial sector catering for the disco type to excess.

Stamp collecting is quite popular and it is not too difficult to find a club.

WALKING AND CLIMBING

Turning now to outdoor sports and pastimes, the fine weather experienced for most of the year makes these particularly enjoyable. I betray my own particular interest by commencing with walking and climbing, and the opportunities for indulging in these are particularly good in the northern part of the Costa Blanca. The recommended months are October to April, as summer is too hot. A few books in English giving routes are available, as well as some clubs for company, as you will see in the local press.

If you can venture inland, why not try walking some of *las cañadas,* as the ancient drovers' paths for sheep are called?

CAMPING

Camping and caravanning enthusiasts are spoiled for choice with so many sites available. So as an alternative to a hurried look at some remote part of the region, take your tent or caravan and explore it at leisure, instead of having to rush home the same day. Shade and sea breezes are the things to look for at the site, as well as the usual facilities.

TENNIS

La Manga has over 30 tennis courts; further courts are available on many of the larger urbanizations.

SWIMMING

Swimming is superb, with so many wonderful beaches and a comfortable sea temperature for such a long season. Many of the beaches are particularly safe for children, as they shelve in very gradually. Even so, there are some beaches with dangerous tides, so take local advice and watch out for the warning flags.

Do not believe the gutter press reports of widespread pollution on the Costa Blanca; most of the beaches passed the EEC tests for an award with ease. A permit is needed for diving.

SAILING AND FISHING

Here again the region is particularly well endowed, with marinas at Denia, Jávea, Calpe (2), Altea, Villajoyosa, Alicante, Santa Pola, and three around Torrevieja.

Fishing is very popular, with good catches being made both from boats and shore, as well as from rivers and lakes.

GOLF

The golf courses cannot rival the unsurpassable excellence of those on the Costa del Sol; but even so, enthusiasts enjoy a round on the two fine 18-hole courses near to La Manga, or the one at Villamartín, just south of Torrevieja. There are also good 9-hole courses at Jávea, near Calpe, and at Altea la Vieja. Not far from Alicante there are 18 holes at San Vicente del Raspeig and 36 at Muchamiel.

CYCLING

Cycling is embraced by Spanish youth, and used by many expatriates for transportation. Because the roads are so narrow, cyclists are a problem to drivers and consequently in considerable danger.

RIDING

Horse riding is not difficult to find at reasonable cost, although it is advisable to keep off congested roads. You would be better advised to take a mountain trek from Altea to the top of the Sierra Aitana.

SHOOTING AND HUNTING

These are both very popular with Spaniards, and their results are regarded as a crop of the land. Areas are generally reserved by a square sign divided obliquely into black and white halves. A licence is required, as it is for the importation of guns. Best prospects are probably on the Isla Mayor, within the Mar Menor lagoon.

BIRD WATCHING

Ornithologists are in for a treat, particularly on the *salinas* between Santa Pola and La Marina, as well as the salt lakes of Torrevieja, both of which are used by flamingos and flocks of other waterbirds.

Pigeon racing is followed in some areas.

KEEPING FIT

Many people want to keep fit to lose excess weight resulting from a fairly indolent life and generous meals. Consequently, groups are formed in many areas to do this together. In my opinion running and jogging in the heat of summer can do you more harm than good; but if you must, then get up early and do it before breakfast.

SKIING

You will have to travel to the Sierra Nevada near Granada for good skiing, or to the Pyrenees.

26

Aid organizations

The Spanish Red Cross (Cruz Roja) is one of the very best aid organizations, whichever country you use for comparison purposes. On the beaches they treat injuries and cuts, besides reuniting the many lost children with their parents! In the water they patrol in rubber dinghies fitted with outboard motors to assist swimmers, windsurfers and people on airbeds who get into difficulties. They operate their own hospitals and have a chain of treatment stations alongside the highway. So they deserve your full support, when collections are made for this deserving charity.

Since the end of the Franco regime, the Roman Catholic Church has lost much of its power and influence. Nevertheless, individual priests can be of considerable help to members of their congregation with problems. Ministers of other religions often find that most of their time is taken up with welfare work; much of this relates to the difficulties of expatriates in settling in a new country, particularly if they are single or bereaved and have the problems of loneliness.

Remember that urbanization committees are there to assist you, although the amount of welfare work which they do may be very limited. However, they often have a great deal of influence with developers and they can be instrumental in solving those disputes and problems which are having a worrying effect, preventing you from obtaining full enjoyment of your new home.

In some areas various community help organizations operate, apart from the urbanization committees. Occasional details appear in the local press, with telephone numbers of volunteer helpers, although if your problem is urgent then it is probably best to approach a church minister or the local tourist office for contacts.

I am certain that you know the type of residents who always seem to be complaining about something or other, and you avoid them like the plague because they spoil your day. Nevertheless, I have always found neighbours to be very supportive to each other and ready to give assistance with any problems or suggesting ways of solving them (expecting, of course, that you will reciprocate if the need arises). So never be afraid to ask your neighbours if they mind watering your garden in your absence, or any other job, as they will be very glad for you to do the same for them.

Hospitalization can pose some problems in Spain, as nurses do very little of the domestic work carried out in some other countries. Normally this is not a great problem for married couples, but it can present a very considerable obstacle for single people, and what small amount of organized assistance, either in hospital or during convalescence at home, that is available is not covered by the Spanish health service or local insurance. This is often very demanding work for one person to do voluntarily, and my advice is to press your urbanization committee to set up a mutual help or volunteer programme for this eventuality.

Geriatric problems can also be severe for single people and surviving spouses. Again, this type of nursing is not covered by the health service or insurance. In cases of great difficulty there may be no alternative to repatriation to the person's home country.

Sheltered homes may be the answer, with care facilities and resident nursing staff. Write to McCarthy & Stone at 11 Queensway, New Milton, Hampshire, who have pioneered the way in this field.

—— 27 ——
Selling a property

I hope that your stay in Spain will be enjoyable, however long it lasts. Should you find that you are unable to settle, or have to sell your property for any other reason, then you will find that the resale property market is rather slow compared with many other countries. Why this should be so, when modern Spanish properties show little sign of previous occupation, is far from clear; perhaps it is because there are so many new houses on the market. Supply and demand therefore results in resales fetching a fair proportion less than new properties, even when they have not been occupied for long.

Many owners sell the furniture as an inclusive package, rather than pay high transportation charges or let it go for a small sum to dealers.

Most vendors will probably employ a local estate agent. Generally they are reasonably effective in reaching prospective buyers in Spain, and their charges are not excessive. In the absence of special circumstances, the seller will not usually need to employ a solicitor. In the past, developers would sometimes repurchase a property, but apparently this is no longer permitted. As an estate agent in Spain often insists on an exclusive selling right, you will probably leave the matter in his hands and not attempt to supplement his efforts.

Vendors who decide to sell their property themselves will probably rely on newspaper advertisements. Likely publications have been detailed in Chapter 8. Alternatively, you may be fortunate in selling the property through your local evening newspaper back home. Organizations which specialize in circulating lists of real estate for sale have been very effective in finding buyers in Britain. This has not escaped attention in Spain, and the *Costa Blanca Property Mart* offers to sell your property for an inclusive charge from £25. Photographs obviously help. Contact Serramar, Edificio Cases Sant Jordi, Altea La Vieja, telephone 584-8019.

The Spanish way of selling is to paint *Se Vende* (for sale) on a wall or a board, together with a telephone number for contact. When in Rome...!

Finally, we come to the matter of transferring the proceeds of the sale abroad, which can be slightly complicated in certain circumstances. Let us begin with the straightforward cases. (In Chapter 9 the importance was stressed of having a foreign money contribution recorded when your *escritura* is registered; the necessity for this will now become obvious.)

If the seller is resident in Spain (or a Spanish national or company), then payment for the property must be made in ordinary pesetas. If no foreign money contribution was recorded, by handing in your *residencia* you change your status to a non-resident; you then have to apply for official permission to open an internal peseta account through a bank, and use the account to purchase Spanish investments. After three years the latter can be sold and the proceeds transferred out of Spain.

Those selling property for medical reasons can make the transfer immediately.

Non-residents do not share all the above problems, as they can sell for any freely-convertible currency, although the buyer could later have a problem when selling if no foreign money contribution is recorded.

If non-residents sell for pesetas, they can convert them to another currency provided that:

▶ their foreign money contribution has been officially notarised

▶ if the sale is to another non-resident, then the buyer has to make a foreign money contribution

▶ the exchange control authorities are satisfied that the sale takes place at the market price, and that you have paid all the taxes which are due

Should the seller not have made a foreign money contribution on purchasing the property, then the above procedure must be followed of applying as a non-resident to open an internal peseta account, which is used to purchase Spanish investments, and waiting for three years.

If the seller had a foreign money contribution recorded, he can export his sale money immediately.

A bank official and a solicitor should be consulted if you are contemplating involved transactions such as buying two properties to sell one and remain a resident in the other, or a series of purchases and sales of various houses.

Try to arrange the timing of your sale so that you are not 'tax resident' for the calendar year in which it takes place. The reason is that if a profit results from the sale, and you do not use it to purchase another Spanish property, then this profit is assessed for Spanish income tax. How do you avoid this? By not being resident for 6 months of the calendar year in question.

Finally, may I warn you not to attempt to contravene the Spanish exchange control regulations. If, on leaving the country, you are found to be carrying large sums in pesetas, not only can the money be confiscated, but you can also be fined or imprisoned.

Appendix I

EMIGRATION CHECKLIST

Moving to Spain is a complicated operation. In order to help you, I have set out below a checklist of earliest and latest dates for completing various operations so that you may timetable your actions, and ensure that you don't forget something. The symbol zero (0) denotes the date of moving to Spain. Negative figures signify the number of days before leaving your home country, and positive ones days after the arrival date in Spain.

Earliest date	Latest date	Action	Date initiated	Date completed
−365	−300	Incorporate your business if it will be sold as a going concern		
−365	−270	Commence seeking a property in Spain		
−365	−270	Start learning Spanish		
−365	−270	Buy Spanish dictionary		
−365	−180	Put your property up for sale		
−365	−180	Read library books on Spain		
−300	−180	Visit property exhibitions		
−270	−90	Book inspection flight		
−270	−30	Buy a stock of cotton clothing		
−270	−30	Make a will in your home country		
−270	−30	Consult Spanish solicitor		
−270	−30	Pay deposit on Spanish property		
−270	+7	Open Spanish bank account		
−180	−90	Obtain a 5 or 10 year passport		
−180	−60	Arrange a school for your children		
−180	−30	Pensioners arrange payment of pension into a bank account		

Earliest date	Latest date	Action	Date initiated	Date completed
−180	+30	Commence a correspondence course, if desired		
−120	−90	Give notice of withdrawal of National Savings Bonds (3 months) and Premium Bonds		
−90	−45	Ask DHSS about your pension contributions		
−90	−30	Arrange documentation to import domestic pets, or find them a new owner		
−90	−30	Renew driving licence, if necessary		
−90	−7	Purchase shortwave radio, if desired		
−90	−7	Buy a Firestone map of your region in Spain		
−90	+30	Buy and read a travel guide to the region		
−60	−30	Purchase reading material, paperbacks, etc.		
−60	−30	Obtain several passport photographs		
−60	−30	Apply for company or self-employed pension to be paid gross of UK tax		
−60	−30	Obtain quotations for storage and transportation of effects		
−60	−30	Open bank account(s) in the Channel Islands		
−60	−21	Obtain tinted glasses		
−60	−14	Close building society and UK (not Channel Islands) bank accounts		
−60	−14	Buy adaptor for 3 pin plug, if required		
−60	−14	Obtain quotations for removal (UK firms)		

Earliest date	Latest date	Action	Date initiated	Date completed
−60	−2	Book flight		
−45	−21	Obtain visa application form		
−30	−14	Sell your furniture		
−30	−14	Arrange credit transfer to Spanish bank account (minimum £250 per person)		
−30	−14	Obtain prescription medicines		
−30	−14	Inform your Inspector of Taxes that you are emigrating and complete form P.85		
−30	−12	Arrange for the disconnection of your telephone		
−30	−10	Obtain Eurolicence or International Driving Permit		
−30	−10	Arrange for your electricity and gas meters to be read		
−30	−7	Arrange storage of effects and keep detailed list		
−30	−7	Arrange payment of storage charges		
−30	−7	Arrange car hire for Spain		
−30	−7	Obtain special visa		
−30	−7	Obtain a supply of Eurocheques, travellers' cheques and pesetas		
−30	−2	Arrange insurance (house and contents		
−30	−2	Place subscriptions for magazines, if desired		
−30	+3	Buy furniture in Spain		
−30	+150	Arrange transportation of effects		
−14	−7	Buy good quality tea to carry		
−14	−5	Buy some British stamps so that friends returning can post your letters		

Earliest date	Latest date	Action	Date initiated	Date completed
−7	−1	Cancel your order for milk and newspapers		
0	0	Obtain *entrada* stamp in your passport		
0	+3	Pay in funds to your Spanish bank account		
0	+90	Complete purchase of property		
0	+90	Pay water and electricity connection plus urbanization charges		
0	+90	Arrange gas contract, if desired		
0	+90	Arrange health insurance (optional for pensioners)		
0	+90	Pensioners register with Spanish Health Service		
0	+90	Obtain fiscal stamps (525 pesetas per person)		
0	+90	Obtain photocopies of passport, house contract and health insurance policy		
0	+90	Apply for *residencia*		
0	+90	Apply for work permit, if necessary		
0	+180	Obtain *escritura* and registration of foreign money contribution		
0	+?	Continue paying voluntary pension contributions until age 60 (if not working) or 65, if desired		
+1	+30	Evaluate cars for purchase		
+7	+14	Contact financial adviser and purchase offshore gilts and/or equities		
+7	+21	Register with consul and obtain certificate of good conduct		
+7	+60	Join sports and other clubs		

Earliest date	Latest date	Action	Date initiated	Date completed
+7	+60	Plan your garden		
+7	+90	Obtain quotations for removal (Spansh firms)		
+7	+90	Obtain confirmation of means from Spanish bank		
+7	+90	Obtain municipal licence if setting up a business		
+7	+90	Arrange funeral insurance, if desired		
+7	+90	Consider life assurance and arrange, if desired		
+7	+90	Make a will in Spain		
+14	+60	Purchase car, arrange insurance and registration		
+14	+120	Consider satellite television		
+14	+365	Obtain Spanish driving licence		
+14	+365	Apply for a telephone to be installed, if desired		
+21	+120	Obtain top soil and start planting your garden		
+60	+150	Collect *residencia* from local police		
+75	+90	Obtain *permanencia* if you have not applied for a *residencia*		
+165	+180	Obtain second *permanencia* if you have not applied for a *residencia*		
+300	+645	Complete Spanish tax returns		
+365	+730	Apply for second *residencia*		

Naturally, individuals' circumstances will vary, and the above can be only a general guide.

Appendix II

USEFUL WORDS AND PHRASES

abogado – solicitor
arrendamiento de temporada – temporary letting for a fixed period
asesor fiscal – tax consultant
ayuntamiento – townhall
certificado literal de nacimiento – birth certificate
contrato – contract
delegación de hacienda – tax office
entrada – arrival
escritura – title deeds
estanco – state tobacconist
franquicia aduanera – duty-free importation
gestor – legal executive
impuesto transmisiones – transfer tax
inmoblaria – estate agent
IVA – Spanish VAT
notario – notary
papel del estado – tax stamps
patrimonio – wealth tax
permanencia – temporary residence permit
permiso de circulación – road licence
plus valía – tax on increase in land value
portador – bearer
renta – income tax
residencia – residence permit
se vende – for sale
tarjeta de inspección tecnica – car identity document

AUTHOR'S NOTE

Readers' comments will be most welcome. Every effort has been made to ensure that this book is up to date at the time of going to print, the manuscript having been checked by members of the legal profession, bank officials and other qualified persons. However, you will appreciate that, particularly as a result of Spain's entry into the Common Market, laws are changing almost daily. Consequently, no liability can be accepted.

In Chapters 15 and 16 an attempt has been made to set out the rather complicated matters of taxation and investment as clearly as possible. If you are still in your home country, then there is little to be done except to delay taking capital gains. Should you have arrived in Spain, if you would like to send any questions on these subjects to the address given below, then I should be delighted to answer them.

Robert H.V. Cooke, FCIS

770 Rosa
Urb. La Marina
E-03194 La Marina
(Alicante)

INDEX

abogodas 46, 53, 91, 93-4, 115-16, 118, 123
accumulation of dividends 81
acquaparks (water amusements) 36
adaptor 119
administrator of community 96
adult education 101-2
Aguas de Busot 18
Aguilas 13
aid organizations 32, 113-14
air bricks 42
Air Travel Advisory Bureau 22
Albaida 102
Albuferereta 20
Alcazar de la Señoría 15
Alcoy 17-18, 29, 37
Alfaz del Pi 104
Alicante 11, 13-14, 17-18, 20, 23, 29-32, 37-8, 53, 57-8, 61, 62, 97, 102-5, 111
  airport 29-30
almond 19, 108
Altea 20, 29-30, 104, 111-12
Altea La Vieja 20, 111
amusement parks 36
Ancla International 30
Andalucia 99
annuities 73
apartments 39
Apolo 63, 86
archaeological museum 17
arrendamiento de temporada 28, 123
asesor fiscal 74, 123
audio-visual learning 97-8
ayuntamiento 15, 17, 53, 93-4, 123
Azar Menor casino 36

bank deposits 74, 82
  interest 72, 76, 82
banker's order 120
banking 81, 88-90, 118-19, 121
banks 48, 53, 58, 93, 116
baptism 93
Barcelona 30-1
Barrio de Santa Cruz 15
Basque 99
BBC World Service 109
beds 50
bed settees 39, 50
beer 34
Benasau 18
Benidoleig 19
Benidorm 18, 20-1, 29-30, 36-7, 57, 104
Benisa 20, 29, 104
Benitachell 104
Biar 17, 102
bid price 77
bird watching 112
births 93
blankets 50
bonds 51, 77, 79-80

books 98, 102, 119
bougainvillaea 106
bridge 110
'bucket shops' 22
building societies 72, 76, 82, 119
bullfights 37
bungalows 40
BUPA 85
Burgos 102
burial 94
business
  licence 66-7
  premises 67
  retirement relief 72
Busot 18
bus routes 29

Cabo de la Nao 20
Cabo de Palos 13
Cabo Huertas 20
cabrito asado 33
cacti 15, 107
cajas de ahorros 88
Callosa de Ensarriá 18, 20, 104
Calpe 20, 29, 104, 111
Campello 20, 104
camping 110
capital
  gains 69, 72-3, 75, 78, 82-3, 123
  loss 72, 78
caravanning 110
carpets 15, 50
cars 61-4
  guarantees 61
  hire 30, 62, 120
  importation 63-4
  insurance 62-3, 86, 122
  purchase 61-2, 121-2
  registration 61-2, 64, 91, 122
  spares 62
  transfers 91, 122
  value added tax 75
Cartagena 13, 17, 29
Casal de San Jordi 18
casinos 36
Castalla 17
Castellano 99
Castillo de la Atalaya 17
Castillo de la Concepción 13
Castillo de la Mola 17
Castillo de San Fernando 15
Castillo de Santa Barbara 15, 20, 102
castles 13, 15, 17, 18, 20, 102
Catalán 99
Catedral de la Marina 20
Catedral del Salvador 15
Catedral de San Nicolás de Bari 15
Catedral de Santa Maria 17
caves 18-19
certificado literal de nacimiento 93, 123
certificate of good conduct 56-8, 121

certificate of registration 57, 66, 121
chairs 50
chalets 40
champagne 35
Channel Islands 72, 76-7, 81, 119
charter flights 22
cheques 88
churches 13, 15, 17, 93
Civil Registry 93
climbing 110
clothing 105, 118
clubs 121
coaches 23
Colegio de Santo Domingo 17
commodities 77, 82
common law spouses 75, 92
communications 30
community
  budget 95-6
  expenses 95
  help organizations 32, 113
  life 95-6
  meetings 95-6
  officers 95-6
  of owners 47, 53, 95-6
  property 96
  regulations 95
  services 96
confirmation of means 57, 59, 122
Confrides 18
Consuls 56-7, 93-4, 121
contract of service 66, 71
convertible peseta account 88
Córdoba 102
Corporation Tax 76
correspondence courses 101-2, 119
Costa Blanca 9-21, 24, 33, 35-6, 38-9, 43-4, 56-7, 65, 75, 81, 97, 99-100, 102-3, 105-7, 110-11
Costa Blanca News 43
Costa Blanca Post 43
Costa Blanca Property Mart 115
Costa del Sol 9-10, 31, 43, 111
cost of living index 27, 67
Crevillente 15, 29, 103
Cueva de Canalobre 18
culture
  shock 59, 95
  Spanish 102
currency funds 77, 79
current accounts 88
customs bonds 51

dancing 36, 110
dated stocks 77
Dehesa de Campoamor 11
delegación de hacienda 27, 62, 74, 123
Denia 19, 21, 29-30, 37, 57, 104, 111
denuncia 66
Department of Health and Social Security 60